I can't get this quietly wonderful book out of my mind and heart. It will not only change your view of adoption, but will radiate outward to change your view of almost everything: marriage, friendship, religion, America. If the deepest human bond is not the accident of birth but the act of commitment, there's hope for this world.

Annie Gottlieb, author of
DO YOU BELIEVE IN MAGIC? BRINGING THE SIXTIES BACK HOME

In this rich and evocative memoir David Jones offers an altogether absorbing account of his growing up in the small-town Northeast and rural Midwest and of family life in many forms. This thoughtful and perceptive book is not just about adoption but about what it means to belong to the human family. Laced with lively anecdotes sometimes humorous, sometimes poignant, always uniquely memorable, it is both a wonderful story and a powerful statement of who we are and how our lives are deeply and meaningfully interconnected.

Sharon Cadman Seelig, Professor of English, Smith College, author of
THE SHADOW OF ETERNITY: BELIEF AND STRUCTURE IN HERBERT, VAUGHAN, AND TRAHERNE, and GENERERATING TEXTS: THE PROGENY OF SEVENTEENTH-CENTURY PROSE

David Jones is a person of great personal charm, intelligence, and human warmth. His memoir of child adoption extends well beyond personal narrative into a broader study of human relations, in which life experience and deep learning illuminate questions of kinship, faith, and marriage. Jones has thought deeply about the nature of choice, offering wise counsels and insights, which will enrich our lives. It is a work of great integrity and clarity that will make its way into readers' hearts, affirming the importance of wise choices as an adjunct to faith.

Douglas Wixson, Professor Emeritus, University of Missouri at Rolla, author of
WORKER-WRITER IN AMERICA: JACK CONROY AND THE TRADITION OF MIDWESTERN LITERARY RADICALISM, 1898–1990

D0920823

My Father's House

My Father's House

✦

A Life of Adoption

David Jones

iUniverse, Inc.

New York Lincoln Shanghai

My Father's House
A Life of Adoption

iUniverse books may be ordered through booksellers or by contacting:

iUniverse
2021 Pine Lake Road, Suite 100
Lincoln, NE 68512
www.iuniverse.com
1-800-Authors (1-800-288-4677)

ISBN-13: 978-0-595-37461-8 (pbk)
ISBN-13: 978-0-595-81855-6 (ebk)
ISBN-10: 0-595-37461-1 (pbk)
ISBN-10: 0-595-81855-2 (ebk)

Printed in the United States of America

To the Memory of my Father and Mother
and
George Blackburn

And his mother and his brothers came; and standing outside they sent to him and called him. And a crowd was sitting about him; and they said to him, "Your mother and your brothers are outside, asking for you." And he replied, "Who are my mother and my brothers?" And looking around on those who sat about him, he said, "Here are my mother and my brother! Whoever does the will of God is my brother, and sister, and mother."

Mark 3: 31–35

Contents

Acknowledgements

Edmund Perry proposed this book, my wife insisted that I write it, and my children thought it was a good thing to do. I want to thank Nick Johnston, Nita Groothuis, Emily Stamos, John Meagher, Al Perkins, Philip and Joan O'Mara, John and Peggy Welty, Harry and Sharon Seelig, Richard Crouter, R.L. Watson, Anne Wilgus Podesta, and John and Janice Bonge for encouraging conversations. John Bonge made a particularly helpful suggestion for organizing the material. Linda Flowers, Steven Smith, Larry Shiner, and Douglas Wixson offered helpful critical readings of the manuscript. Annie Gottlieb, Sharon Seelig, and Douglas Wixson urged publication. My wife Nancy and Daisy Thorp listened and read patiently and advised me wisely. My daughter Margie showed her love for me by typing the manuscript, and Vivian Anderson typed a revised draft. Dorothy Grant provided dependable duplicating services. My son Brooks and Todd Hinson contributed indispensable technical assistance. My daughter Rachel encouraged me by laughing at appropriate places.

I am grateful to my uncles, and especially Reynier V. Jones and Cecil K. Jones, for their part in my life and this book. I owe a special debt to Edward Ouellette, Edmund Perry, Christopher Lasch, and Robert Wiebe. My appreciation for John Coleman Bennett remains inexpressible.

Prologue

In ancient Rome, when a man had sired a child, he acted out a ritual to pledge himself to become the father, and not merely the sire, of that child. The baby was brought to him and placed on the ground at his feet. Then the man reached down to the child to pick it up, drawing it to him and himself to it. In this act he "adopted" his own biological offspring, and the act represents what must happen if we are to be parents and children and not simply the producers and products of human procreation. There is a profound truth played out in that old Roman ritual, one that is timeless and that lies at the heart of my understanding of life.

Introduction

My real father died twenty years ago. I say it that way because I am an adopted son. From my earliest memory I have held those who adopted me into their hearts and home as my parents. They are my mother and my father. This book is occasioned by recalling my father's death, but its source is the life he and my mother made for me. I hope it will summon up and amplify the experience of others: those who are adopted and those who are not. Any experience that rings true is true for all experience. I have not written a clinical study of adoption and the questions it raises and the answers it provides. I have instead set forth my own experience as an example of adoption and then extended its meaning into social, political, and religious reality. My experience was _of_ adoption; my theme is experience _as_ adoption.

At the most immediate level this book is about fathers and sons, and I hope my experience illuminates a very old theme in Western consciousness. It is, of course, also about my mother and me, of whom I have wonderful memories. She made her own special mark on me, both by providing an unshakable sense of security and in special moments and acts of enduring affection. But the simple truth is that my father was in charge of both my mother and me, and the narrative will make clear that he was the primary force and influence in my life. I have written autobiographically, but this is not my autobiography. I have written much of my father, but this is not his biography. It is my story of adoption.

At another level this book is a memoir, and I hope it evokes what it was like to grow up in a small Midwestern town that was really but a village in the 1940s and 50s. But the details of that experience are told in the interest of my basic theme, a theme that finds resonance in various ways. I was adopted by the little town where we lived, by a Sunday School class of grown men, and by the man who worked for my father as caretaker at Merom Institute. This is how it was for me.

I have tried to draw readers along a path I traveled which may be recognizable as their own.

I write also from a perspective strongly influenced by that refraction of Christian faith that came to be my own. I think this grounds my story in an understanding which has universal application, though not everyone will share my theological assumptions. It doesn't matter. What is true is true. The words from Mark insist that at the level of life where it matters most, literal blood kinship is a circumstance, even often an accident, and not a self-evident meaning. Real meaning comes by way of relationship, of meeting, of sharing, of giving: in short, of seeing each other as members of the human family. For Christians, the meaning of humanity is derived from God's love, but my concern here is valid both in and out of the faith.

It will become clear that my father was the center of our family, unmistakably the one around whom my mother's life and mine turned. My mother was altogether a creature of her time and upbringing; women were taught to accommodate their husbands. That was her world. As a Protestant minister's wife the already-imposed cultural model fit even more snugly. Her grandfather had been a Methodist minister, and I have often heard her say that her grandmother used to tell her, "Carol, the job of a minister's wife is to make a home for her husband." My mother believed this and she certainly acted on it. And she simply was not temperamentally given to taking the lead, and my father was. They struck a bargain each understood and accepted, and neither ever regretted it. My father said often, and not only to me, that my mother was his best friend. She said just as often that he was the finest person she ever knew. That was their way in their time. It is not my way, but it is my story.

Another aspect of the story that concerns their time and way is language. We have become peculiarly sensitive, and rightly, to language perceived as sexist and racist. For example, my father characteristically took God to be a heavenly "Father," and believed in and talked convictionally about the "brotherhood of man." So did Julius Hansen, who appears prominently in these pages. The word "Negro" was respectful. Now in our own time this, for many, simply will not do.

I am here neither defending such language nor ignoring objections to it. I am recalling how it was.

My father was one of five brothers and my mother was one of four sisters, and the meaning of adoption for me flowed from our family to their families and back again. My father's brother Ernie married my mother's twin sister Lucy in their mid-forties, and children were not reasonably a part of their future. The other sisters, none of whom bore a child, and their husbands each adopted a child. In her ninetieth year, my mother recalled that friends sometimes wondered aloud what was wrong with the Hughes girls that they birthed no babies. Instead they adopted children, which seemed natural enough to me.

This book is an affirmation, and it is more. It is an essay at clarifying wider meanings by considering marriage, the United States in historical perspective, and the Christian Church. But this attempt to clarify wider meanings is implicit in every line I have written, whether I reflect upon adoption, recount my own experience of it, or recall people and events. These meanings, always, are enriched by my experience as an adopted child as I searched to make sense of life and the world.

We Picked You Out

"We didn't bring you into the world," my father said as I followed him through the kitchen door and into our back yard, "we picked you out." I would hear him use that expression, "to pick out," when he spoke of someone's choosing a mate. I was three years old when we came from Demorest, Georgia, to Putney, Vermont, in the late fall of 1940, and what he said the following summer is my earliest conscious memory: "We didn't bring you into the world, we picked you out." I always knew I was adopted.

The human story is an eternal quest for self-knowledge, and this special knowledge, gathered at the beginning of my understanding, may be the most important thing I ever learned. One of the more poignant manifestations of the human quest is the search for biological roots by people who are adopted. That only a small minority of Americans feel compelled to do this—three percent according to one estimate—makes the anguish and uncertainty of those who feel they must do it no less touching, for to know one's biology is not to know one's self. I do not trivialize anyone's "need to know" when I say that one needs to know that one is adopted. This is saving and defining knowledge. One needs to learn this naturally in order not to discover it unnaturally at what then must be an anxious time in a threatening circumstance.

Adoptive parents are usually distinguished from real parents, which explains why one response to the Delphic Oracle's imperative to "know thyself" is to search out one's "real," that is biological, parents. This is a fool's errand. In no way that matters is it true to say that biological parents are "real" and adoptive parents are not. How do a man and a woman who have brought up a child through adolescence, say, suddenly cease to be "real"? The imputation of "realness" to biological parents is related, ironically, to another confusion, namely the notion that some children are born illegitimate. Does that mean that some children are "unreal"? The irony is that while biology is here assumed to account for "realness" in a parent, that very biology can assign "unrealness," that is illegitimacy, to a child. How can a child reared in an adoptive family be or become "unreal"? Someone has said that there are no illegitimate children, only illegitimate parents, but surely such appointment is not reserved for unwed mothers who may give up a child for adoption. There is an essential biological requirement for getting someone "into the world," as my father used to say. Indeed, that requires a sire and a bearer. But to be a parent is to become a parent, to do the things a parent does in relation to a child.

We muddle meaning when we use language imprecisely, as when we say that a man "fathers" a child. We mean by this that a man supplies a live sperm at the right moment to enable a woman to conceive. We need to speak plainly and we should not say that such a function constitutes "fathering," for it does not. "To father" means to be a father to a child, to do the things one does in order to be a father. The rate of child-support payments in default shows this. When we speak of "mothering" a child, we do not mean "to conceive," but precisely to be a mother to a child. I have never heard a woman use the term "to mother" when she meant "to conceive" or "to give birth." "Mothering" means to be a mother and "fathering" should mean to be a father. When my father told me that he and my mother had picked me out, he told me what I needed to know, as surely as Martin Luther needed to remind himself that he was baptized.

My father was the Congregational minister in Putney for four years, for me a time of childhood and for the world a time of war. In those years I began to feel what it meant to be "picked out," and the intersecting of those personal and public worlds fed my understanding of who I was and why. In Putney I became aware of my mother and father, was thrust upon Sunday School and church, as one would expect for the minister's son, made friends and began school, and began to learn of sex. And even then in Putney I knew the world could be frightening and violent.

I began school at Hickory Ridge, about three miles out of town. My parents felt I was too young to last all day each day of my first year, so when the season and weather allowed, my father twice a week rode a bicycle up to the school to play games with the boys and girls, in return for my tuition, and to fetch me home. He would peddle up from Putney and organize games for us, having as much fun himself as any of us did. He was a natural, and those times were, as Dickens wrote, "conducive to great larks."

The larks concluded the morning schedule, and he would then put me on the handlebars of his bicycle and we would ride downhill toward home. The dirt road ran beside a brook, and almost always he recited a stanza of Tennyson:

I chatter, chatter as I go
To join the brimming river,
For men may come and men may go
But I go on forever.

That was my introduction to formal education and to English poetry. In sixth grade, in another part of the country, when the teacher told us we were to write a poem, I composed some lines I called "The Brook."

There were wonderful times next door to our house in the community center. Women were often at work there on various projects to help the war effort: knitting or wrapping or sending. For the children there were games and the fun of staying up later than usual for evening programs. Sometimes there was roller skating, and my father would scoop me up and put me on his shoulders, weaving in and out of other skaters as he glided swiftly around the floor. My mother worried that he went too fast and was too reckless, but he loved it and so did I.

It was in Putney that Donald Watt founded the Experiment in International Living. My father and mother regarded him as a man ahead of his time, gifted with a true vision of how the world should be. For me, he was the man who lived out in the country and in front of whose house was a pond where I first swam. I waded in that pond and splashed about, and then hung onto my father's neck and shoulders as he swam out into deeper water, fearing but trusting him. When he insisted that I swim on my own, I did, secure in the knowledge that he was there beside me.

If he led me to new adventures and tests of will and spirit, my mother was unfailingly sympathetic and supportive. She was always there. I could count on her to applaud any effort and embrace me for having made it. She did not discriminate in her affection. I came home from school one day to announce with great pride that I had won a ski competition for my age group. I knew it was a scam: the man in charge shoveled together a tiny jump just for me, he counted the distance I rolled after falling down trying to negotiate it, and he placed me in a competition entirely by myself. I knew all this. But when he declared me the winner, I went home happily to announce the good news. My father ignored my triumphant declaration, but my mother hugged me to her, delighted and proud that I had done so well. Here was established a pattern that would hold true as I grew up.

We lived next door to a loud and profane family with three boys, all older than I, who taught me to swear. Later my father would worry about the influence of my Uncle Ernie, his older brother, who refused to modify his language for a nephew. I heard nothing from him I did not learn in Putney. I suspect any minister's child is unusually vulnerable to the language of faith cast in a different key; our neighbors were my initiation committee. They were versed in the sexual and scatological aspects of swearing, as well as in the usual variations on the idiom one heard in church. It took me a while to work things out, because I was now exposed to a vernacular I never heard at home, never in any way, and I did not immediately make all the proper distinctions necessary to preserve that fiction so many American boys must pretend to: that they know only what they have heard at home and must speak nothing else, ever.

I learned I could not take for granted the social innocuousness of street language. When I was four years old, I came in the house one day to find my mother entertaining one of the ladies from the church. I settled in to play on the floor across the room from where they talked, and abruptly applied to the moment what I had been learning. "Mom," I said without looking up, "I am going to kick your ass." I wanted only to share my world with her, not yet realizing that such a hope was doomed. My abrupt announcement failed to stall her conversation, and I tried again. "Mom," I said a little louder, "I'm going to kick your ass." I wanted her to know of my progress in life. This time she seemed aware that I had said something, and turned to ask what it was. With an assured audience I became eloquent. "I said," repeating the phrase with emphasis, "that I am going to kick your ass." There it was, just as I'd heard it so often next door. This time the words found their mark—but only to perplex her.

"Why, I don't understand it," she said. "I don't understand why you said that."

I scarcely did myself, but I felt pleased to have her attention. Her guest also drew to attention.

"That's right, Mom," I sang out, now quite in control, "I'm going to kick you in the ass."

"David, you mustn't talk like that," said my mother. "I don't want to hear you say that again. Now you go play somewhere else."

I usually did what she said, so I got up to leave and went outside. As I made my exit I heard her say to the guest, "Oh, do forgive me, Dear," and then I was out of range. I really did not in that moment grasp either the literal or metaphorical meaning of the expression I had used, but I began to understand that there are some things a child does not say to his parents.

Those neighbor boys, and I guess nearly all the other boys in town I knew, also introduced me to sex. I do not mean I learned from them that mothers are different from fathers and that little boys are different from little girls. Those boys revealed to me a sensibility, come upon early in their own lives, that comprehended sex as something males do to females by whatever means allowed, and sometimes not allowed, and that much of life is meant to be spent trying to do it. I heard the language of sex and began to recognize sexual overtones and innuendoes. I understood now, after trying out the word "ass" on my mother, that this new language was not to be spoken at home. There was explicit Anglo-Saxon reference to girls and boys and men and women, though there was much I could not then understand. It always came, at this stage, from other boys—the stories and jokes and desires and boasts. Here, at the birth of this new awareness, it was always boys and never girls to whom I listened and from whom I learned.

Sometimes a joke or a story was passed along in a knot of boys gathered against the wall in the community center, while adults earnestly clustered about their worthy purposes at tables or out on the floor in the center of the room. Or stories and boasts floated among us as we ran and played about the town: who had done what and who could do what and who would do what.

Privately, the rite of passage for American boys is the capacity to ejaculate. Always, in the jokes and stories and fantasies, ejaculation was prominent. Freud may have been wrong about penis envy, but everyone has been right about male anxiety occasioned by genital size. Boys worry about the size of their penises; they talk about it and make explicit comparisons. As in all things, life is not fair, and some boys are big while others are little. That is the way of it, as girls discover when they grow breasts. For boys, the great equalizer is ejaculation. It may be true with respect to genital endowment that some are more equal than others, but the irreducible fact of semenic ejaculation makes all things fair. And so the capacity to achieve it assumes extraordinary significance in the lives of young males. To "shoot" is to arrive. This was much discussed and displayed in Putney, Vermont.

I made some connection between babies and mothers and fathers, though I realized that my own mother and father had not "brought me into the world." And somehow, there was an early understanding that the things boys talked about doing with girls, especially the older boys and girls, had something to do with babies, at least when big people did these things. But the way it worked out for my childhood's understanding was to create a divide. At home I experienced family without any sexual awareness, as I was coming to be aware of sex. Away from home, I became aware of sex, but it had no relation to family life. The more I learned as I grew older and was privy to the talk of still older boys, the more it was clear that the last thing they wanted was to join sex and family. Home and family were where you tried to mind your manners, and the fun and mystery and anxiety of sex began when home and family were left behind for that world of self-discovery and adventure that required confederates and prohibited parents. My mother and father never would properly bring them together for me.

When I was five or six, the middle son of the family next door took me to a place just beyond the center of town on the highway. It appeared to be a truck stop and a diner. The older boy, who was about twelve, took me upstairs into a room with girls who looked as they'd either just got up or were about to go to bed. He walked right in, as if he knew his way and knew the girls. There was a kind of fearful wonder in this for me. Here was a different ambience. I knew I did not belong; it did not feel right or good or clean. It felt unsafe. These were not the people my parents associated with and among whom I found my way at church. Such young women were new to me even among my friends. I knew I must leave and that I must not report I had been there. The other boy ignored my nervous hints that we should get away from this room and these people, and I could only stay and watch and listen. Nothing happened, but I was aware that the conversation was charged with sexual suggestiveness. He would leave when he wanted to, he said, and we did. I never went back, and I never spoke of it.

Later in winter that same boy smashed up his face terribly in a sledding accident on a sharply curved road which ran down a steep hill near our house. He was so horribly bruised and scarred that my mother would not allow him in our house. He looked, to her, grotesque. It is the only time I ever knew her to be inhospitable. She sought to protect me, but of course I simply slipped next door to see him there. He was, for a while, one of the sights of Putney. Here was an ugly truth, and I was too young and too tender to look upon it. So thought my mother. I would have thought the lesson was to watch out for that hill on a sled. Instead, it was to stay away from a boy who emerged badly disfigured from a winter mishap.

There was more to be learned next door. The father came home one day to be told by his wife that his youngest son, three or four years older than I, had transgressed, and he went immediately down to the basement that was a woodshed. The boy and I had been playing; I did not know what he had done that was wrong, and I could not comprehend what now took place. His father profanely commanded his son to follow him, and I followed too, anxious and afraid. The father ignored me, and as I watched, my friend stood still, knowing from experience what to expect and resigned to it. The father, swearing continuously, searched the wood pile for a board small enough to wield handily and big enough to hurt. The boy had to stand there and watch his father pick up two or three possible weapons and test each one against his palm, discarding them in turn and swearing all the while. Then satisfied with his selection, the man gripped the piece of wood firmly and turned toward his son, still ignoring me, and yelled:

"All right, goddammit it, come here and bend over."

The boy did what he was told. I watched, helpless and horrified and afraid to run even as I feared to stay. The father took his son by the shirt collar with his left hand, and with the board in his right hand raised his arm above the boy and brought the board down across his bottom. This was incomprehensibly new to me, and something I would never know and never forget. The boy was nine or ten years old and the father was a thick-bodied man, and he hit his son with that board. He hit him again and again, swearing as he did, as if the whole thing were an imposition on him and an inconvenience to him, and as if the necessity for it was itself an outrage. The boy yelled and screamed, whether in real pain or because he thought by crying he could purchase mercy, or perhaps both, I couldn't know. The father brought the board down upon him, and he yelled and screamed and squirmed and jerked, and always the father yelled at him:

"Hold still, goddammit, hold still." And then he hit him again.

I was terrified, for myself and the boy. He hit him again and again until he broke the board across his son's lower backside. And when the board broke, he dropped the part of it he still held in his right hand and released the boy from his left hand and said simply, "All right," and went back upstairs. I remained rooted to my spot, speechless. This was a new order of reality. It was impossible that the boy did not hurt. The astonishing thing was that as soon as the beating ended, my friend seemed to treat it as matter-of-factly as had his father. In the act itself father and son were antagonists, though the contest was altogether uneven. The father commanded an instrument of power and inflicted it upon his son in a fit of anger. The boy was his victim. Yet it was clear that the father commanded authority as well. He had felt justly offended and obliged to act as he had according to some code I had no idea of, and apparently the son concurred. He complained neither of the occasion for punishment nor of its severity. It was brutal, and they each took it in stride. It was business as usual as business went in their family, and it was a strange new world to me. Here was a father's prerogative played out upon his son, one surely handed down by his father and one his now-beaten boy would in turn assume when he had sons of his own. Once over, the ritual I witnessed seemed to have no bearing on anything else.

I would hear my father tell me, as I grew up, that his own father had been too rough on some of his brothers. He loved his mother, but he was never happy with his father. He was more than stern, my father felt, he was harsh. He told me often of his own humiliation and helpless anger as his father beat Uncle Rey, my father's youngest brother, unmercifully, and my father could do nothing about it. "The poor kid," he would say as he told me, "I had to stand there and watch. There was nothing I could do to help. He really hurt the kid." Years later Rey characterized my grandfather as "good-hearted."

I believe my father never forgave his father for beating Rey. He may have tried to understand him, but he never got over that beating. He would tell me that his father was "a dreamer," an impractical man who lacked the common sense required to rear a family of five boys. From his improvidence my father learned that debt could be oppressive, and he never went into debt. He never bought anything on time. He used to tell me that all he could remember of life on the farm was working to pay interest on a mortgage. He learned from that and worried about his mother. I think he simply felt set apart from his father. It was partly because his father's impracticality burdened my grandmother. And it was partly because he was so still and unyielding and authoritarian; it was unfair of him "to take my older brother, Ernie, out of school after the eighth grade to work on the farm," my father said. But mostly it was because he beat Rey. He never forgot it.

He never told me anything good about his father, and I cannot remember his saying anything critical of his mother. She was not, as he said, a well-organized person, and had trouble managing a house with five boys in it, but he understood that. He simply endured his father. If his father ever encouraged him in anything, he never told me about it. It was his mother who believed in him and who tried to help him. When he went off to college at Rutgers, on a scholarship that made it possible, his mother gave him seventy-five dollars she had saved a few cents at a time and had kept hidden from his father. "She knew Pop would spend it; it would just disappear," he said. He never missed his father, that I could tell, but he always wanted to visit his mother more often than we did. When his father died, I do not think my father mourned him.

The only good thing I ever heard him say about my grandfather Jones was something he said not to me but let fly in a sermon up in the chapel at Merom Institute. Stung by some poor roof repairs he had just paid for, he was preaching about integrity, and he said emphatically that "my dad would never take pay for a shoddy job." In fact, Grandfather Jones was a skilled carpenter, a craftsman really, from whom Uncle Ernie must have taken some talent and inspiration. He played the cello with considerable feeling, and he sang a fine tenor. I can remember how, when we'd go to the farm, my mother would ask him to play. "Oh, do, Father," she would say, "do play for us," and he would bring out his cello and play a piece or two, unaccompanied. By the time he died, I was the grandchild adjudged most likely to play it, having taken some piano lessons, and the cello came to me. I was completely uninterested in it, and we swapped it for a trumpet in a music store in Terre Haute, when I was fourteen.

My mother always got on well with Grandfather Jones. She would explain to me that his failures as a father, especially the way he punished his children, were a consequence of his own upbringing. "He never knew anything else," she would say, "it really wasn't his fault. He didn't know what else to do." I never knew if he beat my father. He was kind enough to me and my cousins. Perhaps he had mellowed. Perhaps his grandchildren simply evoked different responses from him. He didn't have to live with us, and he was not responsible for us, and he saw us now and then for a little while. Our presence was no implied judgment on his life. And perhaps he was getting too old to care.

When he died, and we were all gathered at the farm to make ready for the funeral, Aunt Lucy, my mother's twin who had married my father's brother Ernie, came in to say that my grandmother had just remarked that Albert hadn't kissed her in twenty-five years. "She wasn't complaining," said Lucy, "she was just remembering it." At the funeral Uncle Cecil, the second youngest of the brothers, whom everyone but his mother and father called "Squeak," was convulsed with sobbing. Rey's jaw was set, and Ernie seemed to me uncharacteristically reflective, but then it was an uncharacteristic occasion. I sat between my mother and father, and he seemed less affected than I was. I remember my grandfather as a very small and slender man with a white beard and a bald head, except for a fringe of white hair. My father always remembered him much younger, beating Uncle Rey. Certain that his father was no fit model for him, he adopted one. He turned Freud upside down.

People talk of God the Father, and we commonly say that our idea of God is some projection or other of our experience with an earthly father. Believers and non-believers alike have tended to speak in these terms. Freud and Feuerbach saw religion itself as such a projection. It is evident that those who have a good experience with a father can more easily imagine a "heavenly father" as a God of love, than those whose human experience has been problematic or worse: one of brutality, violence, indifference, rejection. It may be that a stern human father makes credible an idea of God as a stern heavenly taskmaster. That religion has embraced ideas of the divine based on a projection of human parental experience, authority, and consequence is undeniable.

My father seemed to me to reverse all this. He tried, I think, to model himself as an earthly father, as my father, after the God he understood to be Jesus' heavenly father. He was clearly reacting against his own father—less than affectionately known as "the Commodore"—and just as clearly influenced by the character and personality of those he much admired, such as Harry Emerson Fosdick and Henry Sloane Coffin. The God who indeed expected his children to respect the creation and obey his commandments and live a good and decent life, and yet above all was a God of love and mercy and kindness and forgiveness, this God was my father's model. He looked to God to learn to be a father.

Of course he did not succeed. But who can quarrel with the model? As Thoreau said, in the long run people hit only what they aim at, so we'd better aim at something high. I do not idealize my father when I describe him as I have. I think everyone who knew him, from his brothers to his grandchildren, realized he was something of a mystic—for better or for worse. There was a heavenly aspect to his earthly pilgrimage. At times he wasn't always quite there, and he was notorious for being distracted by the slightest thing. I think this was part of a consciously cultivated spirituality, one of whose purposes was to help make him a better father. Warts and all, as Cromwell said, and he had them, he presented me with a different father from the one given to him.

He and my mother both spanked me. I don't think it troubled her; spanking was, she seemed to think, sometimes necessary. She did it and that was that. I always thought he felt he exposed a flaw in himself when he resorted to physical punishment. He prided himself on patience and understanding, and, above all, on maintaining his composure. He thought the worst thing one could do socially or professionally was "lose your head." If he ever blew his cool with a parishioner or at a meeting or in a social gathering or when leading recreation, I never knew it. He would blow it with me and, I think, feel he had failed himself. The first spanking I remember seems funny now, though it hurt then, but it taught me something.

I learned "Jesus Loves Me" in Sunday School, and one Sunday back home after church I sought to impress my father by singing it lustily, again and again. How could he, the minister of the church, fail to applaud such an earnest spiritual exercise? I chose the wrong moment. He went to the telephone and I marched after, blaring all the way. As he took the call I sang more shrilly. He tried to talk but couldn't and asked me to stop. I didn't and he demanded that I be quiet. Still I didn't. He excused himself, hung up the phone, and then he spanked me. Had I later turned against the church, that moment would have been pivotal. I recovered quickly enough, with some lingering uncertainty about the ways of God and his people, but it taught me something valuable. It is not only what you say, or even sing, but when you do it. I discovered early, taught quite unpremeditatedly by my father, that "ripeness is all," though many years would pass before I came upon Shakespeare's phrasing.

Right alongside "Jesus Loves Me" in early mind and easy memory was "Praise the Lord and Pass the Ammunition." That song joined, momentarily at least, church and state in a way that would have pleased the early New England Fathers. Everyone, especially all kids in town, knew this one: those who went to church and those who didn't. The song served as an agent of national loyalty and identification. Everybody knew it and many loved to sing it, everywhere. But not my father. For him that little wartime ditty bordered on the obscene even as it crossed the line of heresy. And as I came to understand why this was so, I began to realize more fully what it meant to be an adopted child.

My father was no pacifist, but he believed in and preached a gospel of universal human brotherhood and a transcendent God whose will was peace on earth. There was something out of tune in singing "Praise the Lord and Pass the Ammunition" to such a sensibility. So far was he from jingoism that military uniforms and even, at times, the American flag roused him to the suspicion that nationalism threatened even the vision of the peaceable kingdom. His great test was World War II just as I was getting old enough to be aware of it, because that war was, as Studs Terkel has so charmingly reminded us, a "good war." From our present perspective, Korea perplexed Americans and Vietnam made cynics of many, at the very least cutting the ground from any national consensus. And Iraq? But World War II was clear to everybody. Wasn't it?

At Rutgers, my father told me, he was required to take ROTC training or something like it. He never explained it to me, and it always seemed to me incongruous, but I think it was a condition attached to his scholarship. One day the drill instructor loudly and profanely "cussed out," as he put it, one of the boys in the unit. "All he did," said my father, "was to hold a rifle a little out of line as we stood at attention. That guy (an epithet for him) really cussed him out. He really turned the air blue." Of such an experience are world-views constructed. More than anything else, I think, that single incident shaped his view and conditioned his feeling about all things military, even more than a year in Germany in 1930–31. He told me of it too often for me to think otherwise.

We knew there was a war in Europe before we were in it. We knew it in Putney, Vermont, because next door to us lived some English children with their mother. In 1940 the British had determined that they needed to ship some of their children to safety. The United States was one logical place, and people on both sides of the Atlantic went to work on the project, including Eleanor Roosevelt. We had successively two English refugee families, as we called them, next door to us. I could scarcely imagine what they had left behind to come over, but they were a constant reminder that things were not well in the world. When the United States was drawn into the war, it came much closer to Putney, as people sent off sons and brothers and fathers to fight, and die, far from home. Ordinarily I heard our Far Eastern enemy called Japs, and often I heard Germans called Krauts. I never heard my father or mother use either term, except to despise it. Putney men came home on furlough if they were lucky and went about town in uniform. When air raid drills frightened me in the night my mother tried to reassure me, as she did when I woke up screaming with leg pains that had nothing to do with the world and everything to do with growing. And always my father held out the vision of a Heavenly Father displeased by the warring of His children and held out the hope of a better world. Still he was no pacifist.

He believed that "Hitler had to be stopped," and said so. His mentor was Reinhold Niebuhr and not Norman Thomas. Hitler was evil and Nazism was pagan, and it was tragically necessary for the United States to go to war. That was life in its essential ambiguity. Though he never swerved from believing and saying that "Hitler had to be stopped," and he felt the same about the militarists in Japan, though he tended to refer to Hitler, he refused to give up on the God of universal love and redemption he found envisioned in the Old Testament book of Isaiah and incarnate in Jesus of Nazareth. As evil as was Nazism, nationalism could be as idolatrous as paganism, and he would not shrink the human family to Americans and their allies. He would not invoke a tribal deity.

He did support the war effort by investing in United States government savings bonds. If the first thing I can remember is hearing my father say, "We picked you out," the second thing that worked its way into my consciousness was that I would one day go to college. It was assumed. Each week in Putney, usually on Monday when he received his salary, he gave me a dollar and sent me up to the post office to buy ten stamps to paste in a book whose purchase value of eighteen dollars and seventy-five cents could be redeemed for twenty-five dollars in ten years. The government bonds were a sound investment. The dollar came from his weekly salary of twenty-six dollars, our only income. He entrusted it to me for the walk to the post office and the purchase of the defense stamps, Series E Bonds. Knowing his salary, an early disclosure to me which could only bind us more tightly together a family, I knew how valuable that single dollar was.

When I was five or six, I arrived at the post office one Monday to discover the dollar was missing. For a moment I felt panicky: not guilty or ashamed or worried about facing my parents, but panicky. I knew what losing it meant; it was irreplaceable. I methodically searched my pockets to no avail. The dollar had to be somewhere between our house and the post office. Deliberately I retraced my steps, searching intently along the way, back down the main street and then onto the side street where we lived. Nearly back home, I spied it where the street sloped into the ditch, still neatly folded in the small square I had put in my pocket. I picked it up, returned to the post office, and made my weekly purchase on my college education. I was proud, and more than that, was relieved. Had I failed I would not be punished: I was relieved because I had not, by losing the dollar, punished us all.

The patriotism of war bonds was not enough for some. Especially for one man in the congregation who, Sunday after Sunday as the war went on, sat in the back of the church and monitored my father's loyalty, whose universal God was alien to him. The man notified the FBI, and an agent showed up one Sunday morning. Suspicious of what he heard, the agent inquired of some of my father's parishioners, and soon made straight for Beatrice Aiken.

Mrs. Aiken was the wife of freshman senator George Aiken, a popular Vermont governor who would distinguish himself for decades in the United States Senate, and in 1966 declared we should say we had won in Vietnam and leave. Beatrice stayed at home in Putney, as she had when George had become governor. Putney was her place, and there the FBI sought her out to check up on my father. Who could be more reliable than such a lady?

I had heard the story from my parents, and mother took a special satisfaction in it. I heard Mrs. Aiken tell it when, shortly after my mother and father moved to Maine in the mid-sixties, she drove over from Vermont for a visit.

"Well, said Beatrice, "a man came to the house and said he understood I was Senator Aiken's wife, and he wanted to talk to me about my minister, Alan Jones."

"What do you want to know?" I asked him.

"He's been reported to us," he said. "We understand he's been preaching peace."

"Well, what do you expect," I told him, "he's a Christian minister."

That ended it for Beatrice. I asked what happened then.

"He didn't know what to say," she said, "and I told him I was too busy to waste my time."

So far as I know that ended the FBI's active interest in my father's preaching, though the man in the congregation who had notified the agency continued to resent the pulpit presence of a man he was sure was subversive. A few years after that visit in Maine, Beatrice died, and George Aiken asked my father to conduct the funeral service in Putney. Afterwards, he told me, he and George walked through one of the Aiken orchards, the Senator seeking solace in quiet memory.

The hardest thing for him to do in Putney was to ask the church treasurer for his salary. There was no margin in our financial lives in those days; we lived from week to week on just what my father earned, save for the one-dollar investment in my future. The church treasurer knew this, and by tardy attention to writing my father his check each week, he forced him to come and ask for it. It humiliated my father. He had almost to beg, for what was rightly his, to feed and keep his family. I realized this only vaguely at the time. Later I would hear both my mother and father speak of it. It stuck in his craw. She said it hastened our departure from Putney.

My father and mother felt a special responsibility toward the two English families who were our neighbors in Putney. Their husbands and fathers remained in England, one in London working for the BBC. We became quite friendly with these "English cousins," as my mother came to call them. Perhaps because our two houses were separated only by the community center, and perhaps because the English mothers felt secure in trusting a minister's family, but probably because we simply got on well, we were often together, especially the children. I suppose we quarreled and fought as children do, but my recollection is of very fond times with my young English friends. They taught me to drink tea. In 1956 I drank tea again with my "English cousins" in London, and in Welwyn Garden City.

There were others in Putney, Vermont, toward whom my father felt a special responsibility, especially a woman and her two sons who lived in a little house outside of town. The woman was an American; her husband was a German soldier. I remember spending the night with them, and their mother supervising their bedtime prayers. I knew their father was in the German army, and it seemed natural to hear, as they said their prayers aloud, an appeal for their father's safety. That was all, simply a prayer to "keep Daddy safe," and nothing about winning the war. I knew my father was for these people and against Hitler, and I knew that their father was fighting for Hitler and against the United States. Their father was fighting against fathers and husbands of American and English children and their mothers. I never knew whether the prayer of my friends for their father's safety was answered.

Coincidence can become irony, and for the person of faith, chance is providential. Here I was as a pre-schooler and then kindergarten and first-grade pupil, beginning to learn the "basics" in school, and learning much more at home and among friends. My father preached a message of love and forgiveness and tried to act it out by befriending both families, one English and the other of a German soldier. If that was not coincidence and irony enough, he had working with him one summer a Japanese-American seminary student. The sight of a Japanese face in those days was enough to arouse anger and provoke violence. I do not know whether that summer internship caused my father problems, or whether it bore any relation to the FBI investigation of his preaching.

I could not then grasp, as I do looking back, the irony of my friendship with the German soldier's sons and the English children. As the German father was at constant risk in Hitler's army, the English fathers were exposed to steady danger in Churchill's London. I felt no strain playing with children whose families were divided by war. I do not remember that the mothers ever met, though the children may have mixed at our house.

Looking back, it seems fitting that my father and mother embraced both of them and encouraged me to be friends with these youngsters, innocent representatives of the tragedy then raging in Europe, and that they helped a congregation to realize that someone who looked like a "Jap" was not necessarily an enemy but a friend, not only a fellow American but a brother Christian. The English family attended our church, and I think the German soldier's family did not, though the boys and I were in school together. My parents reached out to both sides because they were human beings and because they were frightened and anxious for the future, and because that is the way they were. In my father's house it seemed natural.

Those Putney years furnished my first conscious memories. My earliest is of being told I was adopted. Surely this is part of the reason for my growing up secure as an adopted child, as a "chosen one." To know, from your earliest understanding, that you are adopted, deliberately and consciously sought out and claimed by a man and a woman who want to become your father and mother, is to know something fundamental. All that remains is to experience the love of those two people as father and mother. And such love is always, not only in formal cases of adoption, something to be demonstrated and proven in experience through time. Everyone needs to be loved and cared for, but there is no evidence I know of that links such love and caring in any important way to blood relationship. What <u>can</u> become an issue is identity and self-understanding if one <u>later</u> learns of adoption in circumstances which obviously make it seem that the adoptive parents wanted to conceal the fact from the child. Telling or not telling a child is the difference that makes the difference. And I was told.

Others may feel differently, but I have trouble believing that someone adopted as a baby, loved without qualification, and told from the beginning of his or her adoption, would ever feel a crisis in identity. What makes for an identity anyway? Obviously there is something in the genes, but what is in the blood? Once told, and freely accepted and embraced without qualification attaching to the adoption itself, a child knows more than he needs to become himself. He knows he is part of a family and he knows he is chosen. There is a particular knowledge that lends strength and comfort to one's self-knowledge when one can say as an adoptee does, "I am chosen." It is important to insist that this sense of security and confidence can come only with being told from the first that one is an adopted child. It would be natural enough for a child, growing up, to have fears and doubts about life and meaning if he has been deliberately shielded from the knowledge of his adoption. Why would anyone, especially the adoptive parents, do this? What is there to hide? Is there shame or guilt attached to it? It would be natural enough for a child to wonder about such things if by accident or through some emotional confrontation he discovered that he was, biologically, someone else's child. Of course. But I think this would be true only if he were late to learn it, and, more than that, if he learned it in such a way as to make him think he was not supposed to know. That would change everything.

I learned of adoption from my parents as I was becoming aware of the tensions they felt in Putney, occasioned by World War II. I do not recall either my father or mother saying anything explicit about "blood." But I recall clearly hearing them say, and sensing the same insistent message in my father's ministry, that all human beings are the same because they are all children of God, even if the boy next door was temporarily disqualified because of his badly marred face. My early consciousness was shaped by an awareness drawn immediately from my mother and father that earthly parents are accidental and all the children of the earth belong to one family. Someone not sharing such an explicit religious point of view might desire another rationale, but the substantive issue remains intact. Biology is an occasion; choosing and loving is the cause.

"We picked you out," my father said that summer day in Putney. Nearly thirty years later, for my birthday, my wife wrote a poem. Nancy, too, was born in Georgia, in very different circumstances, and she knew the meaning of what my father said:

Inauspicious birth
Georgia-hot July
Plucked by grace from nothingness
   or worse
And set
In the midst of love
To learn to love.

And that is the truth of it.

Let Her Win

"Remember, don't win."

"What?"

"Don't win. Let her win."

My father was prepping me for our annual visit to the lady who could only be regarded as the patroness of South Willington, Connecticut, when we arrived there in September of 1944. Miss Rosa Hall controlled the town, a small village about halfway between Stafford Springs and Willimantic, and four miles from the University of Connecticut at Storrs. Hartford, which claimed us for an occasional shopping trip, was twenty-five miles away. South Willington, on the Willimantic River, was a thread-mill town, and the mill, where most people worked, was Miss Hall's.

I went to school at Hall Memorial, where I was immediately devastated. My mother restored me. I have said, and my story will make clear, that my father was the dominant one in our family and the paramount influence in my life. But at critical moments my mother was crucial to my well-being, and that was never truer than in South Willington. I had learned to read print with facility, but cursive script was foreign to me. The first and second grade teacher—she taught both in one room—regularly wrote directions on the blackboard which were incomprehensible to me. I could infer that for each line of her handwriting my classmates produced a line in response on their papers. She would direct the class, for example, to "draw eight red squares," or to "make six orange circles." The idea was to pay attention, take written direction, and do the assignment. I was lost; her writing might as well have been Greek or Chinese. I would look around and realize a correspondence in the number of lines on the board and those on pupils' pages, and in desperation I made up things to put down on paper. When an assigned classmate collected our efforts, on receiving mine he or she predictably laughed at it, which I took to be at me. I could read, silently or aloud, as well as anyone in my second-grade class, but I couldn't penetrate cursive. The teacher had to know what was wrong, but she did nothing to help me. When we went outside for a morning recess or after lunch to play, I was so upset I slipped away and ran home, only a block from the school, where I could truthfully tell my mother my stomach hurt or I had a headache, but couldn't manage to tell her why. Each day for a week I huddled on the sofa in her arms and cried, while she sought to discover what was wrong. No one from the school came around to inquire, and I dutifully went back the next day.

At the end of a week I brought myself to explain it all to her, without using the word "cursive" which was then unknown to me. She grasped the entire difficulty immediately, and said brightly, "Oh, I can fix that," and she did. She sat down with me, and in a writing hand which remained remarkably clear until she had a stroke at nearly ninety, taught me to read and write cursive letters. In thirty minutes. It was revelatory and transforming. I owe much to many teachers through the years, but my greatest learning debt is to my mother. I returned to school confident and competent, and never looked back. Neither have I ever found it easy to forgive that teacher, and if she walked in now at age one hundred and ten I might hit her.

The church might as well have been named for Miss Hall's family too. My mother recalled that Miss Hall had it built; it scarcely matters. It was hers. Its structure was not in the fashion of white-steepled New England churches on the green, but more like stones piled up on one another, not ugly, only unimaginative. New Englanders regard a town as Midwesterners do a township, and my father served two churches in Willington, the one in South Willington and next to which we lived, and another one up on Willington Hill which more resembled the picture postcard New England Congregational meeting house.

The Hall holdings made one aware of class, that dirty word in the American lexicon. Names encountered about the town, and not only in South Willington, declared ethnicity. Eastern Europe, particularly Czechoslovakia, was prominently represented by Tomaska, Stuicki, Hukla, Parisak, Venosick, and Wokamurka.

Ravazzo reminded us of southern Europe. Most were worn by second or third-generation Americans who yet remembered with pride their old-country heritage. The Americans lately come from Czechoslovakia loved to dance the polka, and how could such dancing be a sin? No overt discrimination or social ostracism divided the town, and certainly not Hall Memorial School. If democracy means an equal opportunity, South Willington had a democratic school. As for the church, ours was the only one in South Willington, and it gathered most of the community. There the melting pot was at least as real as imagined, heated at every opportunity by my mother and father. Though church was only once a week, they promoted special programs and occasional suppers falling between Sabbaths.

Miss Hall was not a bad woman. Far from it. The issue was power, and she had most of it in South Willington. She was a benevolent despot, good and gentle, but all too powerful. She served her will through the man who had married her niece and who lived in the grandest house in town. My parents and I were dressing for dinner and the evening at the next finest.

When my father had felt it was time to leave the church in Putney, Vermont, he candidated actively for two Congregational pastorates: one on Mt. Desert Island in Maine, and the other in Willington. He could have had either one. He often speculated, though he did not elaborate, on how our lives might have been different had we moved to Maine instead of Connecticut. We didn't. He always said it was my mother's choice, which is ironic, to say the least. He would say that she, having braved the rigors of what must have seemed a foreign land in south Georgia, and having then contended with a sprawling, ill-heated, and poorly appointed house in Putney, now came to what appeared as a promised land: a fully and finely furnished two-story parsonage. Anyone who has lived close to a Protestant minister's wife in rural or small-town America will understand that the most devoted missionary spirit can falter, away from the amenities of home. My father used to say that when he brought my mother and me to see South Willington, she was smitten with the parsonage and said simply, "Oh, Alan." That, he said, did it. We moved from Putney, Vermont, to South Willington, Connecticut.

Once a year at Christmas, Miss Hall, who must have been about sixty years old, invited us to her gracious home for dinner and some Chinese checkers. This was the meaning of my father's warning. Chinese checkers must have been the nearest thing she experienced to riotous living. She wanted her minister and his family to enjoy her table. And she wanted us to join her in her favorite game. So here we were, preparing to go, my mother seeing that I dressed in my best, and my father reminding me once more of my annual duty.

"Let her win," he said, "be sure to let her win. It makes her happy."

I did and we did and I don't think she ever caught on. The real challenge was not mine but my father's. I was a child who impatiently attacked Chinese checkers as I dabbled in other amusements. He was, as in all things, systematic and methodical, nothing if not ordered. He often told me that his nearest glimpse of a perfect world was when he studied geometry in high school. If you learned the rules and followed them, it all came out right. The world of geometry was coherent and harmonious. He applied that vision to checkers, at which he was very good. I knew from experience that for him Chinese checkers was a piece of cake. He could see ahead and visualize the board with various strategies. Always, of course, there was the possibility that someone else would muck up your own little "rabbit path," as he called it. But usually he came out ahead. He was good at it because he could see consequences, was good at games, and had a tough competitive streak which belied his undeniable human kindness. And truth to tell, he liked to win. So his was the challenge, not mine. How could he let the old lady win without making it obvious that he was throwing the game? He did. We took dinner at her home each Christmas season we were there, and each of those times we played Chinese checkers. She always won, and winning always made her happy. She looked the way a child does when it has won favor with a parent. By winning she favored herself.

The children in South Willington knew of Miss Hall as something of a combination of the Pope and the Wizard Of Oz, each become female. She was real. Everyone knew that. Still, one did not often see her. Now and then she would emerge from her house to be driven around the town by her chauffeur, and she must have come to church, though I don't recall it. She appeared anything but impressive, a short and somewhat plump little lady with no compelling features or habits. She was never rude, rather the epitome of politeness. But she lacked warmth and vitality; She could never have been mistaken for anyone's mother, and she could be imagined even less in the arms of a suitor. She was altogether ordinary in appearance. But everyone knew who she was and what she owned. Most of the families depended on the Hall enterprises for their livelihood, and children learned early not to do or say anything which might bring retribution upon a breadwinner. That apparently extended to beating her at Chinese checkers.

The truth was that my father was, to a painful degree, her kept cleric. This is always the case, more or less, in a congregational form of church claiming local autonomy, and this was Miss Hall's congregation. He had an instinct for the underdog, and in Willington that meant, collectively, the working people. Historically it was plain to him that trade unionism was a necessary check on the power of capitalist management. He was for the working people in South Willington, but he used to tell me later that "you dare not say anything about labor unions." He made the best of it by being the best pastor he could, and especially by working energetically with the young people. With the war still on when we went there, gasoline rationing provided a captive audience. He worked effectively, helped by my mother, and they were loved for it. It was plain they wanted something good, and always better, for their working-class parishioners and for their children. But my father preached no social gospel sermons in that church. He'd have been out of a pulpit; it was that simple. I am sure this compromise hurt him, and I suspect it explains best why he decided to leave so soon.

Soon after we moved to South Willington my mother and father considered adopting another child. From friends in Vermont they learned of a two-year-old girl available for adoption. I have the details from my mother's account but I do remember their discussing the possibility with me. My mother said that after they decided against it, but had not yet told me, I called upstairs from the basement where I was playing, "when am I going to have my new sister?" One reason they decided not to adopt the little girl was that she had a growth on her spine "as large as a grapefruit," as my mother quoted the doctor who had examined her. It had been removed but grew back. My parents were uncertain about her physical condition and the future of her health. They were not sure they could provide the care she might need.

My mother often recalled that Miss Hall was adamantly opposed to the idea of further adoption, regarding my father as "her minister" whose time should be spent on his parish and not his family. My mother could attend to that, which meant me, but without adding to the responsibility. My mother remembers that she and I were summoned by Miss Hall to accompany her to Hartford in her chauffeured car, to buy me a snowsuit. That was *noblesse oblige*. An additional child in the family would not do. "She didn't want Dad taking on more family duty," she said.

The main reason they didn't do it was that my father felt he lacked the strength and energy to assume parental responsibility for another child. He was past forty now, and though younger than my mother by four and a half years, he was the one whose health was problematic. I began to realize this in Willington. I knew my father as a man who had ridden me on his bicycle and taught me to swim, and who himself was a strong swimmer who beat high school boys in races at summer camps, who loved to roller skate and ice skate and ski, who played softball with kids and grown men, and who still played basketball. It didn't make sense. How could he lack the strength?

"Well, Dear," said my mother when I asked her, "because he was so sick, you see."

I didn't see. I could remember once in Putney when he had simply disappeared into his bedroom for about a week and my mother had told me we must be quiet and let him rest to regain his strength. I felt, as children do at such times, that nothing could happen to my father, and yet sensed an unnatural anxiety over his condition. He had gone out with the men of the church to cut wood to fire the church furnace, and it had been too much for him. Later I would realize he ought never to have gone, but he had felt a duty to lead and not merely to exhort. I never knew whether he suffered a slight stroke or a mild heart attack, or simply gave way before the strain. After a solemn week of quiet in the house he reappeared in my life and took up his pastoral duties again. That I could remember, and I asked my mother if that was what she meant by saying he had been sick.

"Oh no, Dear," she said, "I mean when he was younger and nearly died."

That was a new beginning. If in Putney I realized who my mother and father were, in Willington I began to learn the history of the family into which I had come. This was the start of it, to be told by my mother that my father had been very ill and almost died.

"It was a miracle really," she said, "that he lived. But that's why he has to take such care of himself and why he must not take on too much."

I went to my father for more. He told me that in his junior year at Rutgers he was fighting to make the starting basketball team. There had been a practice in an old gymnasium without bath facilities, and afterwards, hot and sweaty, he and the others had come out to a bus which was to take them home. He caught a cold which worsened into rheumatic fever, and he wound up in Middlesex Hospital in New Jersey.

"They gave me up for dead," he said, "and I knew that if I was going to die I wanted to die at home and not there in the hospital."

"But you didn't," I said wonderingly. "You didn't die."

"I managed to pull through," he said, "but it was a long hard pull. I had to drop out of school for a year, and then I had another attack when I was in seminary and had to drop out of school again for a year. I tell you, it puts the fear of God in you to come so close to dying."

My father was the second of five brothers. He was born in Newark, New Jersey, and spent his early years growing up in Irvington. When he was fourteen, the family moved out to a farm in Hunterdon County, and he went to high school in Clinton. The brothers were all about five feet eight inches tall, but they varied considerably in build. Rey, the youngest, was the lightest, though strong and wiry. Cecil, called "Squeak," appeared a little more muscular to me than Rey, and Ernie, the oldest, was quite stocky. Arthur, the middle brother, no taller than the others but at 240 pounds probably a hundred heavier than Rey, was immense. Still, you could see that he and the others looked like brothers. Except for my father. There was something different about him physically. He was the same height and had some of the same facial characteristics and the same tendency toward baldness. But something set him apart. Despite his love of sports and exercise, surrounded by his brothers he seemed less physical. I attributed this to his temperament and work. He was a minister. Naturally he would appear more "spiritual" than the others.

My Uncle Cecil recalled him as a teenager and a high school athlete very differently.

"Casey," he said, using the nickname my father had acquired in high school and which Squeak always called him, "was strong as hell. He had a neck like a bull. You didn't want to mess with him."

I began to ask my father about his youth, about growing up on the farm and going to high school and about playing ball. He had done the kind of strenuous work that hardens and broadens and toughens a boy into a man; he had pitched hay and dug ditches; he had played sports: baseball and basketball and track. He ran the half-mile and cross-country. Even now, he still obviously enjoyed games and exercise. Yet he was not robust, as might be expected of so athletic a young man. As I thought about it, I realized he was careful of his health and especially concerned to conserve his strength, even as he played and swam and worked in his garden. Before I could ask he answered.

"But then I got sick."

I could only imagine what he must have been like before his illness. I could look at my uncles and mentally take some years off them and imagine how they were then, as boys and young men. With my father it was otherwise. I knew he had been an athlete, because he could still play ball pretty well for someone his age. But to picture him as physically powerful, as Squeak insisted he had been, required an act of imagination. It was much easier to believe that a woman in Georgia seeing him in bathing trunks, had cackled that she was sure he could sing, "cause you got laigs lak a mockingbird."

"I had a real chance to be on the starting team that year," he said. "I played forward, as I had in high school. I wasn't very big but I was aggressive."

This, too, was new. Though I knew him to be a sharp competitor, I saw him playing for fun at church picnics and pick-up games where everybody got to play. He always thought playing with kids helped keep them out of trouble. He never lost his temper or tried to take unfair advantage of an opponent. His general deportment and behavior were anything but aggressive. He seemed to me even then, and this impression would grow through the years, to pride himself on kindness and gentleness and patience. He had been an aggressive basketball player at Rutgers? My father? The minister?

"Oh, that's when I fell in love with him," my mother told me happily, "when I saw him play basketball. Oh, he was so daring in those days."

"In high school, in Clinton," said my father, "we had a team of boys who played hard and who were in good physical condition. We didn't have any substitutes; you had to play the whole game. We were known as the 'fighting five.' I think we won most of our games because we outlasted the other teams. When I went to Rutgers I wanted to play basketball, and I ran cross-country too. Now that is a test of endurance. I thought it would help me in basketball."

Then he said it again.

"But then I got sick."

It was clear to me later, as I grew up and he grew older, that the illness he contracted when he was twenty years old, and from which he narrowly escaped, was the defining event of his life. Everything subsequent took its place and meaning from it. Where he had been "strong as hell," as Squeak put it, now he was frail. He would spend the rest of his life not only trying to recover from rheumatic fever, but trying to regain some of his former strength and capacity. The most he could hope for was a relatively normal life, free from constriction and pain. This he achieved. The way he worked and the way he played, the way he ate and the way he slept, the way he lived his life, all took on a clearer meaning in light of his illness.

I had realized but had not bothered to try to understand that our lives, my mother's and mine, were considerably conditioned by my father's health. One obvious manifestation that now seems to have served as a kind of metaphor, was that he always took a nap after lunch. I knew he was an early riser, especially in the summer when he liked to work in the garden in the cool of the morning, and it made sense to take a little siesta at midday. Now I began to understand that the condition of his heart, damaged by the rheumatic fever, was the controlling agent in his schedule. He was adjustable and adaptable to the claims of his parishioners, his "people," as he put it, and I rarely saw him impatient with any of them. But he insisted on his nap. Whether he actually needed it or only thought he did, he could not function without it. I learned that the one thing I must not violate was his naptime. He slept for twenty minutes or half an hour. He would undress and lie down on his bed and tie a handkerchief over his eyes. I thought it looked silly, but it shut out the daylight and allowed him to sleep. He could drop off to sleep quickly, and never needed to set an alarm, though my mother was schooled to wake him if he overslept. He rarely did. I was given to know that the most important thing I could do to help him in his work as a minister was to leave him alone while he slept. The cardinal sin was to awaken him. I cannot remember that I ever did, even inadvertently. This was my first sense of making some positive contribution to the life of our family.

Now I realized as well that we ate carefully. My father was convinced that a proper diet could help him live longer. We ate fruit and vegetables, and meat when we could during the war, but always there was fruit. He opposed desserts in principle, by which he meant cakes and pies, thinking them to be harmful to the human system. If my mother wished to serve fruit and call it dessert, that was quite acceptable. The one exception he made was for ice cream. He loved ice cream, and pretended to discourage me from eating it. "You wouldn't like it, Son," he would say, "it's burned." I believed him, and for years I did not like it. He ate it greedily. He never smoked or drank; ginger ale was his limit. He remained a milk drinker all his life. His most profound dietary conviction rested upon the efficacy of shredded wheat. He believed in shredded wheat and rye crisp. Whenever my mother was away at meal time, whatever time of day, I knew what we would eat: good old shredded wheat.

So he had been sick, very sick, and it changed his life forever. It is common to hear that someone faced with imminent death loves life the more for having escaped the grim reaper. It was more than this with my father. He professed and plainly lived out what I can only call a sacramental understanding of life. All was grace and everything good was sacred. That a new day dawned more than pleased him, it filled him with gratitude and delight. He never lost this sense, and I do not believe it diminished even in his later years. The pace would change, and he would have to slow down. But always you saw in him a man immensely glad to be alive and who could not bear to waste a moment in anything frivolous. He did not, he could not, trivialize life. He had come too close to losing it for that. This I began to realize in Willington. It was an awareness that grew year by year, and one shared by many people who knew him. It showed; it shone in his countenance.

What of the miracle that had saved him for such a life of joy and gratitude? He had said he didn't want to die in the hospital, but I hadn't heard the rest of the story. Now he told it to me and in later years would return to it. After my father died Uncle Cecil told me what happened. He and Uncle Rey and I had driven over to Frenchtown, New Jersey, for lunch in July, 1984. As we approached the little cafe where we would eat, Rey pointed out the baseball field where, he said, he had played his best high school game.

"I had two singles, two doubles, and an unassisted double-play."

"Did you win?" I asked.

"You bet," he laughed, "we beat the hell out of them."

After lunch as we drove out of town, Squeak said that the doctor who had saved my father's life had come from Frenchtown to the farm to treat him.

"Old Doc Grimm," he said, "he saved Casey's life after they gave up on him down at Middlesex Hospital."

"I'd forgotten the name of the doctor," I said.

"Easy enough to remember," said Rey from the driver's side. "Just think of Grimm's fairy tales."

"That really was a fairy tale," said Squeak from the back seat. "It was a miracle that Casey lived. The doctors at the hospital thought he didn't have a chance, and Casey said if he was going to die, he wanted to die at home. So Ernie got a truck and put some bed springs in the back to make a home-made ambulance, and went down to get him."

I had forgotten this, too. It came back to me as Squeak told it. Ernie rigged up and fitted out the contraption he needed to do the job, as he so often did, and in honoring what everyone thought was a dying wish, helped bring my father back to life.

"He lived sixty years after that," I said. "That's remarkable."

"It was a real miracle," said Squeak, with as much reverence in his voice as I had ever heard. "Doc Grimm was a wonderful man. When he died, the whole town shut down."

I never understood just what Doctor Grimm had done when he came to treat my father, unless it was to give him hope that he might still make it through the crisis. He told me once that the Frenchtown physician had said to him, "Alan, the human body is a great and wonderful mystery. We really don't know much about it." Whatever "it" was that old Doc Grimm "did," Squeak had it right when he said what my mother had told me, that it was a miracle. And that miracle that gave my father back his life made life itself a miracle and a wonder for him that was impossible to miss. To grow up in my father's house was to be taught and shown that life is precious and each day a sacrament.

"And then I got sick again," my father said.

He had graduated from Rutgers in 1926, a year later than the class with which he entered, and enrolled at Union Theological Seminary in New York. He had been inspired by the minister in the Methodist church his family attended when he lived on the farm and went to high school. He knew, he would tell me, he wanted to work with his head and not his hands. He might have made a career of teaching. I think he felt he could do the most good as a minister. Union appealed to him because it was inter-denominational, attracted an international student body, and had an outstanding faculty. He suffered another severe attack of rheumatic fever during his third year there. This illness, too, was long and serious, though I don't think his doctors gave up on him this time. It cost him a year of convalescence, and when he graduated in 1930, in a class that counted such people who would distinguish themselves in theological scholarship as Paul Lehman and Joseph Haroutunian, he won a fellowship to study in Germany for a year at the University of Halle.

The strongest influences at Union came from Henry Sloane Coffin, the president, and Harry Emerson Fosdick, his theological hero. Coffin was, to him, a perfect Christian gentleman, a rigorous scholar, and an effective administrator. He came to see my father when he was sick in the hospital. "I don't suppose he was there more than ten minutes," he would tell me, "but I had the feeling that he gave his complete attention to me." Then and there, my father said, he learned how to be a pastor. Fosdick was then waging his battle against the fundamental-ists and making himself heard as the most distinguished preacher in the United States. He taught a course in Bible at Union which captivated my father. He had already read some of Fosdick's books, and he used to tell me that the one which made the strongest impression on him was *The Manhood of the Master*. He took it with him to the field when he worked on the farm, plowing or cultivating, and when he reached the end of a row at the edge of the field, he would pull it out and read a page or two while he "gave the horses a blow." These two were the paramount influences on him and became his models for the Christian life in contemporary America. Until Reinhold Niebuhr came to Union.

There is no way adequately to convey the impact Niebuhr made on his students. He invested his exposition of ideas with a raw energy that itself was compelling. More than anyone else it was Reinhold Niebuhr, himself fresh from a now famous pastorate in Detroit, who influenced my father to go to south Georgia during the Great Depression in order to serve the Lord with gladness. Later my father would say to me that "Old Reinie" challenged you to "get out there and serve." Ironically, had my father's health remained intact and had he graduated with his class from both college and seminary, he would never have encountered Reinhold Niebuhr at Union. Niebuhr arrived in the fall of 1928, just after my father would have graduated, had he not become ill.

When he came back from the year in Germany he took a job with the Board of Home Missions of the Congregational and Christian Churches. He went down to Waycross, Georgia, to serve four rural parishes. He had grown up in a Methodist Church and attended an inter-denominational seminary. He might have cast his lot with a different denomination. It was the particular job that attracted him. He had an opportunity to take a church in Chapel Hill, North Carolina, a university parish that would have stimulated and challenged him intellectually. He chose south Georgia with Reinhold Niebuhr's challenge spurring him on: get out and serve.

Early in 1932 Rey drove down to Georgia to bring him back to New Jersey to marry my mother. They had met while he was at Rutgers and she at the New Jersey College for Women, now Douglass. She was older than he, but had entered college late, and that made them undergraduate contemporaries. They met at a "Christian social," and she often recalled how he came up to introduce himself and said, "I'm Casey Jones." They became and remained friends for the next four years, including the time of his illness. That put him a year behind her as she prepared to graduate in 1925 with a Phi Beta Kappa key she laughingly said she didn't deserve. He planned to attend all the events and ceremonies surrounding her graduation, but then told her on a spring afternoon that, as she remembered it, "it was all or nothing," and it could not be all just yet. So it must for now be nothing, and he broke off their "friendship." He was still in school and had no means of support and that was that. His version of that time and those decisions was rather different. He always insisted that he asked her to marry him but she couldn't make up her mind. She said he never really asked, but just announced that the time wasn't right.

She remembered quite specifically when he did ask her to marry him because it was Columbus Day: October 12, 1931. She was teaching in New York state and he had gone down to Georgia to his Home Missions parish. He came back to New Jersey expressly to seek her hand, and called at the Hughes home in Watchung. Her mother and father called her up to tell her he was there. She had planned to come home for the weekend anyway, as she remembered it, and when she arrived he asked her to marry him and she accepted. Because she was under contract to teach for the school year she had to request a release, and by the time she worked that out and made the arrangements, an April wedding was planned.

She brought to the marriage an equal dedication to serving God and doing good. She only wanted, she says looking back, "to be a missionary." Her view of it was simple and altogether unsophisticated; she wanted to help needy people. Her background was somewhat more cosmopolitan than my father's. She was born in Jersey City, but her father removed his family to Watchung in 1907, when my mother was eight years old. Carol Hughes was a twin, born on Christmas Day, and my father always called her his Christmas Carol. Her father was a distinguished New York newspaperman, whose most spectacular triumph was, as city editor of the *New York World*, to break the story of the sinking of the *Titanic*. Later he would write a regular column for the *Wall Street Journal*. Her mother was very efficient in the house and in the garden, and exceptionally musical. All her daughters were musical, my mother least of all, but she may have enjoyed it the most. She studied both piano and voice, and her greatest pleasure in life would be to direct church choirs, especially children's choirs.

It is an understatement to say that nothing in my mother's life up to that point had prepared her to be a home missionary. She had taken graduate courses at both Columbia and NYU, and tried teaching for a few years. She was not then successful; she would return to it after I went to college, and prove very good at it. Both she and my father saw in each other someone of high ideals and sincere commitment to a cause they both embraced. My mother told me often that what drew her to my father above all else—though she loved to say she fell in love with him when she saw him play basketball—was that "He was the finest person I had ever met." She had been quite dominated by her father, who now told her that he and her mother thought it would be a good thing for her to marry Alan Jones. So she did, and for the next half century and a bit more, he took over where her father had left off. They were a splendid team at work in the ministry. Dozens and hundreds and even thousands of people saw that and gave thanks for it. If my father was the finest person she had ever known, for his part he regarded my mother as "the best friend I've ever had." No marriage is perfect, as none is made in heaven, but theirs was a good match. No one has been more grateful than I.

They lived in Waycross and served four churches out in the country. Home was a little apartment for which they paid ten dollars a month and ten cents a bath. That meant, says my mother, that "it was a treat" to take a bath, one they enjoyed but "not every day." The most remarkable thing about their ministry was that they were both Northerners who were accepted and loved by "their people" in those Southern rural parishes. They imagined themselves, or at least he imagined them, to be latter-day disciples of Jesus, sent out two by two to preach the good news and to try to make life better for those who would hear it. They had little to live on and few material resources to work with, but I have heard him say he thought they "did more good" in those early years than at any time later on. They were confident the will of God was done.

The most dramatic experience of their south Georgia years, one my father never spoke of but which my mother told me about many times, and always with fierce pride and admiration, ironically involved another man named Jones. Fred Jones had been threatening to take over one of their four little churches, declaring it was God's Will and that no one would deny him his calling. Fred Jones may have been deceived about the will of God, but he was deadly earnest about carrying out what he took it to be, and he spread tension and fear through the church and the community. One day when my father went calling on some parishioners and did not come home on time for lunch, my mother became worried, fearing that Fred Jones's group had caught up with him and done him harm. More than fifty years later she remembered her anxiety. She went across the street to a friend who was a school teacher, who drove her out to where my father had said he was going. He was fine and could not understand, says my mother, why she cried when she saw him.

One Sunday morning Fred Jones and his men came armed into that little country church during the worship service and demanded that my father come down from the pulpit. He stood his ground, says my mother, and without raising his voice tried to carry on with the service. Fred Jones and his bullies swaggered about the small sanctuary, waving their pistols in the air and threatening my father. My mother says some of the congregation were frightened for him. She was. But, she says, her voice still strong with admiration, he showed no sign of fear and would not play the coward. He was the minister of the church, and the Congregational tradition gave the congregation the right to determine whether he would remain. He said so, and declared that he and my mother would wait outside for the congregation to register its will. If the people desired, he would remain as the minister, and, he implied, take his chances with Mr. Fred Jones. If the congregation voted him out, he and my mother would take their calling elsewhere.

This is my mother's account; my father never spoke of it to me, even when I asked him to. He refused abruptly to discuss it. I think he felt it would betray a pride he would not acknowledge were he to talk about it. They walked out the door of the church and into the pine woods where they sat on a log. He told her the vote might go against them and they would have to leave these people. He seemed to be apologizing to her for such a possibility, but she assured him that whatever came they would see it through together. Never, she says, did he seem afraid, only uncertain of the outcome. I have asked her if she felt afraid for herself, and she didn't remember.

The congregation did vote him out as the minister. But my parents were not left alone. About thirty members came out to join them there in the woods, and a new church was born. They worshipped for a little while on logs outdoors a few miles away. Then a doctor gave them some land and the Home Mission Board transported a frame building down to Waycross from South Carolina. The grateful congregation named the church Williams Chapel for the doctor who gave the land on which it stood. Some of the happiest memories my mother and father took with them from Georgia were of the new fellowship formed with those loyal people who followed them into the woods that Sunday morning. There is no record that the church Fred Jones took over at gunpoint ever prospered in the sight of man or of God.

My father and mother moved north to Braselton, Georgia, about sixty miles from Atlanta, and again served four rural churches. Here they lived in a little two-room house that had been used to store feed for turkeys. He painted the rooms white, and got sick from doing it, and later they newspapered an adjoining lean-to and used it as a kitchen. Here, in neighboring and equally tiny Hoschton, in July of 1937, they adopted me, just before moving once more, this time to Demorest, up in the north Georgia hills.

My father was the minister of the local Congregational Church, and he also taught Bible and philosophy at little Piedmont College and served as college chaplain. I spent my first three years in Demorest, but remember nothing of it. My mother says I spoke my first sentence there, at fifteen months. She came outdoors where I was playing to see if I needed to go to the bathroom, and I said, "Mama, don't bodder me." I must have learned it from my father.

Now in South Willington, I was learning where I had come from by way of
adoption. A family history is absorbed, but it must be appropriated to make it
one's own, whether blood kin or adopted. Their story became my story, and after
I came into their lives and they into mine, it was our story. I was the first grandchild on my father's side. Art and Squeak followed with children; Rey's were born
to his second wife after the rest of us left childhood. Ernie and Lucy married late
and had no children. No distinction attached itself to my adoption. What did set
me apart was that I was an only child and a minister's son. Ernie sometimes introduced my father as his "Holy Joe brother," and at meals would remark, "you can
say grace if it'll make you feel better." My Jones cousins never slighted me because
I was the son of a cleric, but they made it clear that it was better I than they.

We were not much alike, but we got on well. The boys—especially Squeak's
sons Barney and Whitey—were all more mechanical than I. In this we reflected
our fathers. Mine was least interested in how things worked, even though he had
adored geometry. He cared for ideas and people. He used to tell me that on the
farm whenever anything went bad, everybody depended on Ernie to fix it. My
father never learned anything much about pumps and motors; he preferred
books. After his death when a library was named for him at Merom Institute in
Indiana, Rey wrote me that he and Squeak remembered him with his nose in a
book more often than not. Art could make an engine run, though not as skillfully
as Ernie, and Rey was a good carpenter. Squeak was a gun nut, who became a
skilled bullet molder. You could see the brothers together, as I did at family gath-
erings, and easily pick out my father as the one most different. You could see by
looking that he wore the white collar.

My uncles might have shunned me because I had neither interest in nor talent
for fixing things and making them work. They didn't. Each made me his nephew.
That my aunts loved me was predictable. Women are supposed to care about
babies and children. Here were strong men who liked pistol shooting, two of
whom saw military service during World War II and two of whom swore pro-
fusely, who took me in and made me feel at home. If they seemed different from
my father then, in retrospect they seem even more so: in interest and temperament and reason for being. They could be gruff and abrupt, but they loved me.

Without apology, without exception, without qualification, and quite without regard for my adoption, they made me a member of the family. I could not do some of the things their children could, and I was a poor pupil when the uncles sought to instruct me in some skill, but there was never any doubt about their affection and their commitment to me. Ernie, the gifted craftsman, took me down to his basement workshop again and again to show me something he had built or repaired, and tried to explain how he had done it. I was always uncomprehending. He would shrug and go back upstairs until the next time. I must have been a disappointment to him, but he was not to me. It wasn't his fault that I cared nothing for what mattered to him. I sometimes spent a few days with Rey and Ruth, and they always took me somewhere, to a movie or a ball game, sometimes to see Rey play baseball.

Children need grandparents and I knew all of mine. My father's mother was ineffective as a homemaker, but she was generous in spirit, and I early saw why my father felt such affection for her. Grandfather Jones seemed less connected to me than Grandmother, not because he scorned me, but because by the time I knew him he seemed often in a world by himself, dreaming of what might have been. There was never any question about my claim on him or my grandmother. There was no asterisk beside my name in the book of the family.

Grandfather and Grandmother Hughes were, according to Uncle Squeak, "true Christians, people who lived it." My mother fondly recalls her father's sense of humor. I liked him. It was clear that he brooked no nonsense, from children or adults, but he was kind even as one deferred to him. Grandmother Hughes was very accomplished domestically, musically, and socially. She managed the household, wrung the necks of chickens to be cooked, and gave her four daughters a love for music. If she ever scolded me I don't remember it.

When I first came to Watchung, Lucy, my mother's twin, who was a nurse, lived at home and worked in New York. She had met Ernie and invited him to make the Hughes house his home and to become a live-in jack-of-all-trades. They married after my grandfather's death in 1945 and built a house just down the hill from the Hughes family home. The match between my mother's twin sister and my father's older brother seemed an improbable one, but it succeeded. Ernie was steady, reliable, and unusually gifted with his hands. Lucy was neurotic, an accident waiting to happen. No one remembers how often she wrecked a car or broke a bone. Once she said to my mother, "Carol, you never break any bones." She was not a happy person and she never, as we say, "found herself." I had a special affection for her because she seemed to have one for me, and because she called me "Chum." She was quite certain my mother would spoil me and, in the fashion of childless sisters, offered expert advice on the rearing of children.

Aunt Helen and Uncle Casper Blackburn had adopted my cousin George, as a baby. He was eight years older than I. Helen, sixteen months older than my mother and Lucy, was an actuarial specialist for a life insurance company in New York, and commuted to Manhattan five days a week for twenty-five years. She loved it. She was the classic commuter, up at precisely the same time each weekday, allowing so much time to dress and eat a quick breakfast, and then so many minutes to drive to the station in Plainfield, where she caught the train and joined a bridge foursome that played until they reached Jersey City, where she took the ferry across to Manhattan and then the subway uptown to her office. Her husband Casper Blackburn came from Omaha and a tradition of naval service. He had been disabled in a fall on a ship and worked out of their home just up the lane from the Hughes house as a free-lance journalist. "Blackie" talked to me as if I were older; he assumed I could manage a conversation worth his time. He was a great baseball fan and helped introduce me to an understanding of the game. In 1950, the summer before he died, he took my father and me to Yankee Stadium to see Joe DiMaggio, past his prime and only a year away from retiring from the game, but still possessed of that special grace no one else ever gave to baseball.

We were often in Watchung during the Christmas holidays, and always up at Helen and Casper's house for Christmas morning. Once when we were opening presents there, I found a toy gun and holster. My father did not approve of guns, even toy ones, but I was an American boy and wanted one. He watched me unwrap the gun and run to my mother to hug her and thank her as she smiled happily for me. She didn't like guns either, but she wanted to please me at

Christmas. She helped me strap it on and I wore it the rest of the morning. He never mentioned it.

My mother's sister Catherine, younger by fourteen years, and her husband Michael Hoffman sometimes joined us in Watchung, and once Catherine came to see us in Willington. She cooked spaghetti for my eighth birthday party. Years later she and Mike adopted my cousin Peter.

My mother and father, their mothers and fathers, my father's brothers and their wives and children, and my mother's sisters and their husbands and my cousin George—especially George as we grew older—were my family. From all of them I learned that kinship means not blood but something acted on and acted out. Willington's meaning for me was that while we lived there I discovered my family.

In the spring of 1947, the war over and most of the brothers and sons and fathers come home to resume their lives in a little New England town we had lived in for less than three years, my father decided it was time to try something else. He would take us out to Indiana, to another little town, this one on the banks of the Wabash River. Miss Hall seemed perplexed that he would want to go so soon after coming to South Willington. Why flee Eden for the wilderness? I think Huck Finn had the answer. Like him, my father, with my mother and me in tow, lit out for the territory.

The Only Place on Earth

"He thought this was the only place on earth, and he'd been in the army, done two hitches and been around, but it was Merom for him. When he got married, he lived in Missouri and he liked that all right. They do have some pretty places there. But there's no place like Merom."

Merom, Indiana, perches on the highest bluff along the Wabash River, halfway between Terre Haute and Vincennes. Established as a river town early in the nineteenth century, it was for a time the county seat, but gave up the courthouse before mid-century. Merom was on the very western edge of the county, and the state, and lacked the advantage the railroad gave to Sullivan. In 1859 Union Christian College was founded on twenty-seven acres on the south edge of town less than a hundred yards from the bluff. This institution struggled into the twentieth century, but finally collapsed in 1924. In 1936 it was resurrected as Merom Institute, a rural-life center under the auspices of the Congregational and Christian Churches. We went there in the spring of 1947 where my father took up a double assignment: Director of the Institute and pastor for the remnant of our denomination who worshipped in the Merom Institute chapel. Merom, named for the Biblical Merom and meaning "high ground," claimed a population of 499 according to the 1940 census. It may have been down to an even 400 when we got there, some of whom remembered Merom's grandest moment: the day early in the century William Jennings Bryan came to town to orate at the Merom Bluff Chautauqua. It didn't matter. Merom became an entire world.

In his book *The Wabash*, William E. Wilson wrote that "to know America, you have to take a good, long look at the Wabash River." Merom people are sure the place to stand to take it is on their bluff, and Nancy and I did that again for a picnic in July of 1985. Drue Pinkston, for years Merom Institute's chief cook, now eighty-eight, was recalling her son who had died of cancer, and how he had loved this place.

He had reason. A park two hundred feet above the river, equipped with a bandstand and picnic tables, and at the edge of the bluff a stone wall at which to stand or on which to sit and enjoy the prospect, allowed a magnificent view of the fields and prairies of eastern Illinois. When the Wabash rose above its banks and flooded the low land on either side of the river, you could marvel at the power of nature and wonder whether the farmers whose acres were under water really believed, as was said, that the bottom land was so rich from periodic flooding that an occasional yield was worth the years the river was out. Cocky Daniels, who operated the hardware store on Main Street, saw the water overtake the lower parts of houses built on stilts on the Illinois side, and said that God never intended for anyone to try to live there anyway.

Down the bluff angled foot paths, improved during the WPA days and irresistible to the young, especially newcomers. A dirt road, sliced through the bluff, descended along the north side of the park to the river's edge, where a flat barge ferry, powered by a Ford engine in an attached skiff, connected it to the Illinois side. Colorful locals captained the Merom ferry, none so memorable as Hoad Wills, who could have given my Uncle Ernie a lesson in language.

Olan Vickrey, who had been born in Merom and lived there all his life of three-quarters of a century, ate lunch with us that day. It had always been Merom for him too, and now nearly forty years after my mother and father brought me to Merom, I asked him if he remembered what he used to tell me about this place.

"What's that, Dave?"

"You used to say, Olie, that you look around here in Merom and see all this beauty, and you just can't understand why anyone would want to start a war. Do you remember how you told me that?"

"Yeah, that's right Dave. It sure is. I still don't understand it."

The thing most prominent in memory, as I recall growing up in my father's house on the banks of the Wabash, was the way he and my mother employed the first-person plural and possessive. I came of age in a home that was ours. So was everything else. It was always our car and our money. I never, never heard my parents refer to money in the singular possessive. It was always our money, as it was our car and our home.

This reality contained two dimensions: privilege and responsibility. An only child is often taken to be indulged. He gets the whole haul of loot at Christmas, for example. The other side of it was that it fell to me to do whatever needed tending, indoors and out. Early on I took up dishwashing, and there was no one else to hide behind when my father wanted help in the garden. It was our home, our money, our car. It was our work to be done.

Toward the end of our first year in Merom, as spring broke over southern Indiana, something vastly more important broke over me and became a defining moment in time and experience. My father loved to garden, and he quickly realized that here he could cultivate, in effect, a small truck farm from which he could supply the Institute kitchen with produce for much of the summer season, helping to feed those attending summer conferences. Fresh vegetables would taste better and cost less. The work was more than enjoyable; it re-created him. It evoked his past and confirmed the sacramental quality of life which so possessed him. He loved to talk about working up a good sweat by getting his hands in clean dirt. These were immediate realities and signs of transcendent favor. He grew a garden because it was meet and right so to do. The hymn writer could have had him in mind:

Sweet the rain's new fall
Sunlit from heaven,
Like the first dewfall
On the first grass.
Praise for the sweetness
Of the wet garden,
Sprung in completeness
Where his feet pass.

He had the land for a large garden beside and behind our house. A square, two-story, eight-room brick structure with a front porch adorned by brick and wooden columns, and an enclosed back porch where we descended to the cellar through a trap door, it stood on the corner of the last intersection on the southwest side of town. A large maple framed it on the north side, and two maples and a walnut tree stood sentinel between the sidewalk and the street in the front. Just across from the northwest corner of the twenty-seven acre campus of Merom Institute, the house faced the town's main street four blocks south of the school, drugstore, post office, and other enterprises that marked the center of the village. The town's back street ran along the bluff and bent away from it at a right angle to continue past the north side of our house. Behind our home stretched land owned by Merom Institute that extended about two hundred feet back to the edge of the bluff and then descended sharply another two hundred feet to the river. A substantial plot on the south side of the house awaited my father's attention. This land, covered with good topsoil that nourished peach and apple trees, made his dream a reality. The land and a garden tractor.

That machine changed my life. Propelled by a gasoline engine which required hand-cranking, like a lawn mower, it could be equipped for cultivating or discing. One guided it by two handle grips, again like a lawn mower but farther apart. It was ideal for working a plowed garden. My father bought it in the spring of 1948 when I was in the fifth grade.

That April was far from "the cruellest month". It was glorious as the days warmed and March winds gave way to soft stirrings which carried the sounds of birds and the scent of growing things. A farmer had plowed the ground, and in those days of lengthening light the soft earth joined touch and smell in clean dirt. I ran home from school to find my father, who knew when to expect me, in the garage preparing to take the new gadget out to the garden that would, months from now, offer up potatoes and corn and tomatoes and green beans. I didn't even go inside to change clothes.

I watched him crank the engine and followed him as he took the little tractor out to the garden. I still watched as he took it down the length of the plot, north to south, and then came back again. He repeated the circuit three or four times, then pulled back the lever that took the machine out of gear to stop its forward motion and said, "All right, Davey Boy. It's all yours. You take it now." I gripped the handles and pushed the gear lever forward and guided it down the garden next to where he had just been. Down I went and back I came, discing the ground, sinking over my shoes into the freshly plowed earth, getting dirt down in them, and caring for nothing but the sheer joy of taming the territory. He stood there for a while to see that I was all right, and then he left me alone in the garden with the tractor while he went about another task. He reappeared in about three quarters of an hour and said, "That's enough for one day. We'll get out here again tomorrow." I was ten and small and he was careful.

It went on that way for the next few days. Gradually he reduced the rounds he made before turning the job over to me, and just as gradually lengthened the time he left me to do it. My mother sometimes came out of the house to watch. Early in the second week of this new dispensation I ran the four blocks from school in my usual five minutes and went straight to the garage to find my father. He was putting gasoline in the engine tank, and said I could crank it and get started when he had finished. He had always done that, starting the engine and taking it out to the garden and making at least one round down and back before giving it over to me. It took all I had but I got it running, guided it out of the garage and out to the garden, and went to work. He watched me all the way, and left as I started down the row. I felt wonderfully independent. Predictably, he reappeared in about an hour and waved me in with a grin. I took it back to the garage as he walked beside me, pulled it out of gear, and shut down the engine by depressing a metal strip against a spark plug. He seemed pleased.

"Good job, Davey Boy," he said as I stepped back from the tractor.

"You know, Dad," I said, "when you get so you can trust me, I can come home and do this by myself, and you won't have to worry about it. I can save you the trouble." I was not testing him or baiting him. I meant that it made sense for him to break me into this routine gradually, as one learns to drive a car or to operate any piece of new equipment. He had been completely supportive, always patient and helpful and never critical. Still that is how I said it: not when I'm bigger or better or older, but when you get so you can trust me.

"I trust you now, Son."

I came home from school after that and helped myself to the little tractor. My father took a picture of me one day as I walked behind it. It shows me from the left as I look hard ahead, more like eight than ten. He always said that it was his favorite picture of me because I look as if I'm going somewhere. He told me that for the rest of his life. But what the picture recalls for me is what he said that April day when the ground was soft and the earth smelled sweet. "I trust you now, Son." I had trusted him when he rode me on his bicycle from Hickory Ridge, and when he put me on his shoulders to roller skate next door in Putney, and when he took me out into Donald Watt's pond to learn to swim. Now he gave it all back to me.

The strangest thing I ever heard my father say was that "nobody ever died in his sleep." I remember hearing it often as I started up to bed. I would say good night to my mother as she played the piano in our living room, and to him as he read in a chair by the fireplace. She would respond with "Good night, Dear," and he, without looking up from his book, would sometimes say as I climbed the stairs, "Nobody ever died in sleep." Why would anyone say that, something obviously inaccurate, especially to a boy on his way to bed? Was he trying to reassure me? I didn't fear the dark, I felt safe in our home, and I had no apprehension of death before morning. Was he reassuring himself, having lived with a weak heart since those critical struggles with rheumatic fever? He had told me of the night back on the farm when he was twenty and Ernie had hauled him home to die, and the family huddled in his bedroom for the deathbed scene, and he felt so tired that he wanted only to sleep. Perhaps that night in his own life, when he slept and did not die but recovered and lived on to greet each day as a gift, prompted his sometime remark to me that "nobody ever died in his sleep." Still, it was strange.

I never heard my father swear. Men who otherwise swore freely guarded their language when he approached. He remarked that ministers are too often seen as tender-minded and not up to hearing rough language or a racy story. "We are the ones who are there when people are dying," he said. "We're not sissies." I was very careful in his hearing, and hoped always my friends would be too.

Except for one night when I was twelve or thirteen as I played poker at our kitchen table with a boy three years older. Only the kitchen light was on, and the house was quiet except for our talk.

"I just love to cuss," said my friend as he dealt the hand.

"Do you?"

"Yeah. Don't you?"

I wasn't sure. We had heard each other swear.

"I guess I do."

"It makes me feel good."

With that he began to display his religious, scatological, and sexual repertory. I joined in. The neighbor boys back in Putney would have been proud. My friend asked, belatedly, if anyone else were home. I assured him we were alone, and we struck it up again. Again he wondered.

"Are you sure nobody else is here?"

"Yeah."

"Where's your dad?"

"I don't know, but he's not here."

"See if he is."

"Dad?" I called loudly.

"What?"

It was low but firm and came from the sofa in the darkened living room where he was lying down. In that moment I knew the meaning of "dead silence." My stomach knotted, my throat constricted, and I was what the Scripture calls sore afraid. I looked horror-stricken across the table at my friend who had dropped his cards and was sliding sideways off his chair towards the door. He never looked up or back.

"I'll see you, Dave."

I was alone with my shame, my guilt, and my father. He neither rose from the sofa nor said anything. I felt trapped in the house and convicted by his silence. To retreat to my room seemed the only appropriate escape; I would have to walk past him to reach the stairs. I got up and moved quickly. "Good night, Dad," I said without pausing.

"Good night," he said back to me as I went right up the stairs.

He did not mention it the next morning or ever. That silence was one of his great achievements as a father. Years later I asked if he remembered and he said he had no recollection of it. That was once, I thought, when he didn't say "nobody ever died in his sleep."

The only question among my friends I can remember arising from my status as an adopted child concerned not my birth, but my parents' sexual activity. Children quickly learn standard social proscription, and sex was forbidden. It was not untried, only unallowed. A long tradition in the Christian Church was alive and well in the congregations to which local families belonged: the tradition of seeing sin and vice in personal terms and equating them with sexual behavior. The very words "morality" and "immorality" bore unmistakable connotation. This was made explicit and everywhere implied. To be sure, you were to tell the truth and not lie, and you were brought up to disdain profanity. But at the heart of "being good" was the demand of sexual abstinence. While the double standard was assumed, whereby girls bore that special responsibility to remain pure and at the very least preserve their honor, even boys, expected to be boys, indulged in sex at the expense of religious rectitude. Sex and religion have long been linked, and the mid-twentieth century culture of Merom, Indiana, did nothing to drive them apart. They could talk all they wanted of Moses and Joshua and even Jesus, but we knew the message: don't do it.

Therefore, because I was adopted and because my father was a minister, while we were young it was not unnatural for us to assume some sexual abstinence, or some spiritual triumph over bodily appetites, presumably sanctified by the institution of marriage. I remember extravagant speculation by some of the boys, generally deriving from the assumption that a minister and his wife who adopted a child must have done that because they wished to refrain from sex. I cannot recall hearing the suggestion that my parents couldn't have children. In fact they didn't, and my father once said they never knew why, physiologically, but indeed they tried. That never occurred to any of us.

My father failed utterly at instructing me sexually. Except for a brief and clinical excursus prompted by my second-grade disingenuous inquiry about babies, my mother never tried. In some ways they were a marvelous example. I early learned that the human body was neither evil nor something to be ashamed of. My parents enjoyed dance; ballet, they felt, was a human response to a divine impulse. My mother often twirled and flitted about the house affecting the movements of dance, and she is so remembered affectionately by friends who were there. Nakedness was not wrong or embarrassing. The body was natural and good, and within the nurture and security of the family, one was un-self-conscious about it. We were often naked to each other. But sex? Even that was a gift of God to a marriage. "There is nothing wrong with sex," I heard my father declare from the pulpit in the chapel at Merom Institute. "I thank God for my home." He had also let out from the pulpit that he "never kissed Carol before we were married." My parents were quaint and never more so than when my father sought to instruct me about sex. There he failed painfully and comically.

"Living things reproduce, Son," he said, as if announcing some grand conclusion, "Living things reproduce." I was twelve and thought I might get a lecture on nature or gardening, or perhaps even the wonder of God in the glory of creation. But no, this was an attempt to mount a topic sentence on sex. "Yes, Son, living things reproduce."

"Listen, Dad, if you don't want me to work in the garden, is it all right if I go play ball?"

The sentence would not be ridden into a paragraph. He had located both of us in his study, where he may have felt more secure in launching the subject, and when he spoke he was leaning back in his swivel chair as he did when he talked with anyone there. He had that familiar look on his face which manifested a serious attempt at reflection on life's great meaning, contending with an appearance of emotional and intellectual trepidation. You never knew what might come of it. He had a terrible time trying to be serious without becoming somber and, at times, funereal. He might have been horrified to realize this, but such self-knowledge, so far as I could learn, was never his. Now, having declared with semi-mystical conviction that "living things reproduce," and having been asked a direct and altogether immediately practical question in response to his metaphysical unveiling, he sat for a moment leaning back with his hands clasped behind his head, wearing his green eye shade and looking down, and, I can see and realize in retrospect, feeling hopelessly out of his element. He just sat there without moving, saying nothing. The desk was but a symbol of the distance between us. It was too immense to be bridged. Then, without looking up or changing his position, he conceded.

"All right, Son. You run along and play ball."

Thus ended my first encounter with the facts of life according to my father. I do not exaggerate when say I got the hell out of there, out into the sunshine of God's world and the security of companions who knew quite well that living things reproduce and that boys and girls did it.

He tried again a year later when I was thirteen. Again we were in the study, he barricaded behind his desk, leaning back in his chair with that grave and yet uncertain look upon his face, and I before him, trying to honor the commandment to honor my father even as I knew how fruitless the conversation would be.

"You may have noticed, Son," he proceeded, "that corn pollinates."

I had, of course, noticed nothing of the sort. I had spent a good deal of my life helping to plant, tend, and harvest corn in his garden. I was familiar with the term pollination, and I had perhaps some imprecise notion of what it meant, but that was all. That I had "noticed" that "corn pollinates" was less inaccurate than irrelevant. Has any American boy ever noticed that corn pollinates? What I had noticed was my father's inept attempts to talk with me about sex.

"Yeah, well, it sure gets hot out there in that corn patch," I said. "Dad, do we have to grow so much of it?"

"Son, what I'm trying to tell you is that everything has to reproduce in life and in nature, including corn. And for corn to reproduce it requires the process of pollination."

What really embarrassed me was that he was so obviously reluctant to come to the point. Even now I wonder if anyone else has ever sought to discuss the facts of life with his son by introducing the pollination of corn.

"You understand what I'm trying to tell you," he said, still leaning back his chair with his hands clasped behind his head and that comically grave look his face. "Everything has to reproduce, and with corn it requires pollination."

I had a sudden impulse to laugh but knew I shouldn't. I could just hear some of my friends, if they ever heard of this, talk about pollinating their girl friends.

"It doesn't just happen," he went on. "There is a process nature has worked out. With corn, it's pollination."

I felt very awkward. I wished for some way to help him to the point. It seemed such a burden to him.

"You see, Son, my dad wasn't very good at explaining things to me," he said. "We were out there on the farm, my brothers and me, and we just didn't know very much about these things."

I understood. They all knew a good deal about nature and things reproducing and probably even corn pollinating. But that is not what he meant to be talking to me about, and though neither of us could come out and say it, I understood his meaning when he said, in an only apparent contradiction, that they didn't know much about these things.

"Did you grow much corn?"

"Well, yes, we had some there on the farm."

He hadn't moved. He was still leaning back in his chair looking down.

"Your buddies probably want you to play some ball." he said.

"I'll see you, Dad," and I was gone.

It was no use. He was unable to instruct me in the physiology and morality of sexual behavior. He could not enunciate a useful idiom; he could not bring himself to be direct. Looking back, it is clear that one of the more frustrating aspects of his personality was a large leaning toward indirection. There was something of the mystic in him, and he was easily deflected from direct communication. Someone would ask him a question and he would appear to evade it. He was roundabout. We kidded him about it as he grew older; he could laugh about it then. The subject of sex probably exacerbated this tendency.

But that was not all. The simple truth of it was that he tried to spiritualize the whole thing. Ideally, people were not charged, much less afflicted, with sexual drives and frustrations. Summer camp and Sunday School and the right sort of Christian atmosphere in the home were supposed to take care of all that. He was a great believer in good and healthy recreation and fellowship. He and the others

who presided over our spiritual welfare and growth at summer church camps simply didn't talk about sex and sexual development. They talked about clean living,
and what a splendid model Jesus was and how important it was to learn to pray.
For my fourteenth birthday he gave me Harry Emerson Fosdick's book on *The
Meaning of Prayer*, as if that would help. It was understood, ever and always, that
to be good—which meant religious—was to remain chaste. There was a never-
never land quality about it. We are born to be sexual creatures, but you could not
have known that from the vast majority of spiritual guides and religious leaders
under whose tutelage generations tried to grow up. There was sex education
aplenty, and often among those attending summer church camps. It came not
from adults but from one's peers, and the language, however inexact, was unmistakable.

When I say his language was vague and indirect, I do not mean only that my
father failed to use the familiar Anglo-Saxon terms or American slang. I mean
that clinical terms such as "sexual intercourse" and "virgin" were not employed.
The best he could do was to move from living things to corn to human beings
who reached the point at which they were "capable of becoming parents." That is
how he said it. Of course I knew what he was driving at, but because he could not
say it, he lost the chance to try to convey a meaning, and that is what I regret. If
one cannot name it, what authority is there for trying to instruct someone else in
responsibility?

My father could laugh at himself, but he could not laugh at sex. I cannot
remember him or my mother ever saying anything funny about it. Humor is
indispensable for coming to terms with one's maturing sexuality, and it was
absent from his discussions with me. I mean, of course, intentional humor. His
attempts to instruct me were hilarious, but not because he meant them to be.

Later I came to think my father assumed a Victorian sensibility precisely to
exorcise some sexual demon. His problem was with himself. There were suggestions of it in letters he wrote to me in college; he did not see how I could date a
girl he thought was beautiful and maintain a proper relationship. In a later letter
to me such suggestions became a plain accounting.

I had finished my second year at Union Theological Seminary, and took a southern Illinois parish for the summer. I lived alone, three or four miles out from the town, next to the rural church I served. My father worried that I would become lonely and do something foolish. He wrote me a letter in which he recalled how, as an exchange student, he had "walked the streets as a lonely kid" in Berlin. Actually, he was far from a kid then; he was past his mid-twenties and had survived two near-fatal attacks of rheumatic fever. Most revealing was the nearest thing to a confession I had ever heard from him, that he had to resist, on those streets, the temptation presented by prostitutes. As he had prevailed, so, he implied, must I. This indeed was more direct than talking of living things or corn pollinating. A few days later he called to ask anxiously whether I had received the letter.

"Yes," I replied, "it came a day or two ago." That was the only honest thing I said.

"I've been uneasy about it," he said. "I wrote some things perhaps I shouldn't have. I've been worried that you'll take some of it the wrong way. I don't want you to think I don't love you."

"I didn't understand it," I lied.

"That's fine," he said, sounding much relieved. "Just forget the whole thing. I'll try to do better next time."

"O. K., Dad, whatever you say." I never forgot the letter or the conversation. I cannot say that I did the right thing, but I thought it was the best thing. I didn't want to embarrass him. Looking back, perhaps he was offering an opening to talk man to man in a way we never had. Perhaps this was his way, to admit to having been tempted by prostitutes in the streets of Berlin, of saying we all have clay feet and parents aren't perfect. Perhaps I missed my chance and so did he.

In one glorious moment, much later, he swept aside all the indirection and silliness of those disastrous attempts to talk about sex during my adolescence and young manhood. After the birth of our third child Nancy and I decided that I would have a vasectomy, and called to tell him and my mother about it. He called back a few days later. He wanted to be sure I was not about to forfeit sexual activity. I explained that the only change would be in the elimination of sperm from my semen. Absolutely nothing would be impaired for either of us except my capacity to impregnate Nancy. This much relieved him, and he spoke for the only time plainly and naturally to me about sex. "I just wanted to be sure you weren't going to sacrifice yourself," he said, "or Nancy. She needs a sex partner too." I assured him once more. "You know," he continued, "Mom still enjoys having me come over and share a bed with her." He was sixty-seven and my mother seventy-two; they had slept in twin beds since I could remember. Then he said something for which I loved him then and bless him now. "After all," he declared very matter-of-factly, "the greatest pleasure you can have is an ejaculation." His confidence was wondrous and grand, and sadly in the way of moments, it didn't last.

Five years later, now in his seventies, as he sat by the lake in Maine outside the home he loved, he looked off toward the sunset across the water and revealed to Nancy and me how unresolved his own sexual self-understanding must have been. I had published an article in the Methodist quarterly *Religion in Life* on Martin Buber and D. H. Lawrence, arguing that much can be learned from Lawrence which can illuminate an understanding of Buber. Lawrence was too much for him; he could not manage the sex.

"Well, what do you think?" I wanted to know.

"Yes, Daddy Alan," said Nancy, "how did you like Dave's article?"

He looked off across the lake.

"Harry Fosdick was a gentleman," he said, "and so was Henry Sloane Coffin."

"What did you think of it?" I tried again.

"Yes, Harry Fosdick was a gentleman," he said again, "he was a gentleman."

Nancy tried to help.

"You did read Dave's article, didn't you?" she asked. "I hope you liked it."

The sun was down now, and I wondered if we ought to give it up.

"Harry Fosdick would never do anything that was not respectable," he said, and almost immediately anticipated an objection to "respectable" by amending himself. "He would never do anything to be ashamed of."

He was like Captain Queeg on the stand in the court-martial scene in *The Caine Mutiny*, and I felt sorry for him. He was coming unraveled over an article I'd written which forced him to look again at himself. I plunged in.

"Alan, what the hell are you talking about," I demanded, rather less than honestly, for it was apparent he was talking about himself. Here was this good man, beloved of so many to whom he had been such a fine minister, unable except by indirection once more to confront the demon. To pretend not to see what was happening to him I thought was the kindest thing. He couldn't face any direct discussion of the meaning of human sexuality, much less by way of D. H. Lawrence. The article had challenged his Victorian heroes, Coffin and Fosdick, and confronted his own persona. I was not the problem and neither was D. H. Lawrence, and I was no longer a boy and could not relieve him by running out to play ball. Nancy was alert to his feelings and announced that we ought to join my mother inside. She and I got up to go in while my father just sat there, still looking out over the lake, as if he were trying to call back the sunset. Neither of us had to tell the other it was sad, or that we would try to do it very differently with our children.

Some days later, when we had returned to our home in Rocky Mount, North Carolina, he and my mother called us, and he brought up the article, though not our conversation.

"I read your article again," he said. "It's a great article."

He never mentioned it again and neither did I.

When Grandfather Jones died in June of 1951, the five brothers converged on the farm just outside Quakertown in that time-honored way of sons, to decide what to do about their newly widowed mother. There was a late lunch the day before the funeral, for which the main fare was a huge and steaming bowl of green beans. I was hungry and curious. The women set the table and waited on the men, while Grandma puttered about the kitchen. The brothers knew when the time had come to get down to business, and Squeak and Rey, each with an emphatic gesture, waved "these kids" from the room. It was time for the male adults to have it to themselves. My cousins left obediently to play outdoors. I continued to eat hot green beans, still hungry and still curious. There was something here that I must know. Squeak informed one of the wives hovering near that no women were now needed, but thanks for the food. I was across the table from Ernie, who had tended to me in the middle of the night when I was a baby.

"Him, too," he said brusquely, "get him out of here too. We don't want the kids here." He looked directly at me. There was no meanness, only impatience. My father, sitting next to Ernie, seemed untouched by this. He was lost in his own meditation and probably assumed that when I finished eating I would leave. Ernie knew better.

In that moment I felt only disappointment. There was no anxiety and no sense of rejection. I knew this was the way of men at such a time, and I wanted to stay with the men. Arthur was sitting next to me. By far the biggest of the brothers, he was also, as Rey once described him, "frighteningly strong," able to lift off the ground a piece of machinery none of the others could budge. He was loud and impulsive, given in youth, according to my father, to putting on a clean shirt or even a new suit of clothes, and then crawling under a car to see what needed to be fixed. He yelled at his kids; he may have yelled at the fares on the bus he drove in Newark. But I knew Arthur was a good and generous man. However loud, he was uncontrollably affectionate. I had seen him hug and kiss my mother and the other women at family reunions, and heard him offer to help fix something that was broken. Never mind that everyone else looked beseechingly to Ernie at such moments, for he was the one with the craftsman's touch, and Art might make it worse. Still, his heart was always in the right place. I had heard him sing when Rey sat down at the piano and played by ear old favorites and long-learned hymns. Art loved to sing in his rich baritone, and to assure everyone that "when it's all said and done" we could depend on his latest idea, which nobody ever did. Just now, across from Ernie and my father, my Uncle Arthur gathered me in his huge arms. I felt nearly swallowed by his overwhelming physical embrace, and he spoke still holding me and looking across the table at Ernie.

"Let him stay," he said "Dave's one of us."

I was nearly fourteen and it was simple and direct and forever.

In August of that same summer on another visit to New Jersey, my father took me to Ebbets Field in Brooklyn to see the Dodgers play the Giants. Ebbets Field was more than a ball park; it was a cultural shrine. The most casual fan knew that

a Giant-Dodger game was more than baseball. It was a test of faith and a valida-
tion of life's purpose. Perhaps nothing in the history of American sport matches
the Dodger-Giant rivalry in the early 1950's. Those were the Dodgers Roger
Kahn later celebrated as *The Boys of Summer*, and if they had not already achieved
a kind of immortality, Kahn's book, a meditation on mortality, raised them to it.

1951 was the year of the "miracle of Coogin's bluff," the season the Giants
overcame a Dodger lead of thirteen-and-a-half games in August to force a three-
game playoff and win the pennant in the final inning of the final game on Bobby
Thomson's home run. The day we went to Ebbets Field to see the Giants invade
the sanctuary of what Kahn would call "the most glorious team that ever played
baseball in the sunlight of Brooklyn," the Dodgers were approaching their biggest
lead.

My father loved New York. All my life I had heard about Nedicks and the
Automat and those two wonderful symbols of unity and brotherhood that faintly
prefigured the coming of the Kingdom of God: the Church of All Nations and
International House. That was how the world was meant to be, he was sure. As
we rode the subway to Ebbets Field I could see that he was glad to be back. He
had lived on a farm during high school, had spent his life in country and small-
town churches, and yet remained fascinated with the energy of city life. For all his
love of solitude and rural sunsets, the sounds of the city captured his imagination.
He loved the variety of speech and accent, and I think he thrilled to its pace: the
rapid, rich, and excitable sounds of city talk, and especially New York City where
he had lived and studied and worked, and whose special "international flavor," as
he liked to call it, nourished his sense of the world as a neighborhood. He
remained a theological liberal, sure that within the jungle of a modern metropo-
lis grew warmth and goodness, and that its cultural and ethnic variety assured
vitality. He had often told me that working with young people on the Lower East
Side, while he was a student at Union, convinced him that the rough and loud
and tough and profane surface of city life concealed ordinary human beings with
ordinary hopes and fears who longed for attention. He really believed shrieking
horns and slamming brakes and incessant cursing announced, heard aright, that
everyone was a child of God waiting and wanting to be baptized into the grand

fellowship of human love and understanding. I thought it was there for him that day packed among people on the subway.

"Well, Dave," he said as we walked from the train and Ebbets Field loomed up less than a block away, "you'll see him today."

"Yeah, we'll see 'em all," I said. "Boy, the Dodgers and the Giants. In Brooklyn. Wait'll I tell Jerry."

"Jackie Robinson," he said. "Today you'll see Jackie Robinson."

Later, when I thought about it, I wondered why he didn't say that <u>we</u> would see Jackie Robinson, but when I thought more about it I knew why. This was for me, for the future my generation would make.

"Yeah, he's really good all right," I said.

"Now you'll see him," said my father, as he selected a ticket window. Very matter-of-factly, as he reached into his wallet and we got into a ticket line, he said, "I want you to see him."

Our seats were in the lower deck grandstand just up the line from third base about a dozen rows back. The vendors were everywhere.

"I may have told you," he said, "that when I worked down on the Lower East Side, I took some boys to see Babe Ruth play at Yankee Stadium. They wanted to touch him," he said, "they just wanted to touch him."

One of the teams was taking infield practice, and I began to identify the players. I knew them all by box score and baseball reputation.

"I want you to see Jackie Robinson," he said again.

Robinson got no hits, but that day I saw and heard and felt an excitement only he could generate. When he reached base on a walk, an emotional electricity charged Ebbets Field. My father turned around to ask a lean black man of about sixty sitting behind us, "Do you think he'll try to steal?"

"That's my belief," said the man solemnly, as if he were confessing his faith. "Yessir, that's my belief."

For black people Jackie Robinson plainly represented a new chapter in the story of American life. Everybody else knew this too, which is why Jackie Robinson was never only himself the man, or Dodger number 42 of those boys of summer, but always and essentially a symbol. Campanella was black, and Irvin and Mays, and some other players on each roster. But Robinson was different, was special, was the testing and the meaning of America, as Gettysburg had been almost a century before. My father knew this and wanted me to know it.

It hardly mattered to the man behind us or to the crowd that Robinson did not steal that day. His being on first base changed forever the game for the teams and the fans. As Jackie Robinson darted on and off the bag, it was as if black America had finally made it to first base, and once there knew the promise of advancing.

In September of 1980 on a visit to Watchung, my cousin George took me to church with him, the church where my mother and father were married, and introduced me to Bobby Thomson. I had no idea that Thomson lived in Watchung or that he knew George or that they went to church together. I did know he had played minor-league ball in Rocky Mount and was sure he would respond to someone living there. He did, and recalled for George and me how it had been—where he had lived, how it was to be in Rocky Mount, North Carolina, as a minor-league ball player, and even some fights he got into. He much preferred this to talking about his famous home run. In March of 1981, ten years after his book and thirty years after I had seen his boys of summer play in Ebbets Field, I met Roger Kahn at the Raleigh-Durham airport and drove him to Rocky Mount for a symposium on "Sports in America" at North Carolina Wesleyan College. He inscribed a copy of *The Boys of Summer* by wishing me "many golden summers in the years ahead."

By the time I was growing up, the ritual of fathers playing with sons, as a primary way of relating to them, was firmly in place, and my father took seriously his responsibility. To be sure, when the garden called, that had first claim on his time; he tried to convince me that such work was enjoyable. I learned patience and discipline and responsiblity, but never then understood how he could enjoy it so. That it was worth doing and had a useful consequence was clear. But the generation gap seemed secure when I would hear my father say as he worked in his garden, "This is my baseball."

We played ball together. He would come home from his office at the Institute day after day in the spring or fall and say, "Let's hit some out." He would get the softball and bat and my glove and he would hit me flies and grounders on Stelle Johnson's lawn just across the street on the north side of our house. We both loved it. At those times I never imagined there was anything else in the world for him to do. Whatever prompted him to do it—he wanted to please me, he needed some exercise, it reminded him of the days when he played ball—he gave himself to it totally and peacefully. Now there were no "headaches," as he called the administrative, financial, and personal problems he must deal with. The world grew small around us and there were only the two of us in it, nobody else, father and son, playing ball together and knowing that just then the world was as it ought to be.

In the winter we'd go up to the gym at the Institute to "shoot baskets." Not to "shoot" or to "play" but to "shoot baskets." Again, I did most of the running, retrieving errant shots as we played "horse" or "21." At first I was too small to get the ball up from beyond the free throw line. My growth was charted by a steadily lengthening range, and my skill by improved accuracy. He would say, "You're about to catch me, Davey Boy," as I made a shot.

And I was. Once I could move out to his shooting range, it was only a matter of time before I caught up to his shooting ability. And then one day as we "shot baskets" I more than caught him, I passed him. We played "horse," and if I shot first I made it. When he made a shot I matched it. After the game, my father said decisively, "Well, you've gone around me now. I can't keep up with you any-more." And he couldn't. But that is the way of fathers and sons, and he wanted me, eventually, to outdo him, as I think fathers generally want their sons to attain higher levels of achievement than they have realized. That is the American Dream. The pause in that moment of recognition does not betray a father's envy of his son, for there is pride in the son's new eminence. It is a pause that recalls what once was, in some now distant time of glory, revealing that time has worked its way more swiftly than it should have. Still, there is ambivalence.

The great symbolic moment of the passing and claiming of the torch came not while my father "hit 'em out" to me or when we "shot baskets," but on the sidewalk that ran in front of our house and past the front garden up beyond the neighbor's. I was fourteen, and nowhere nearly as strong and fast as he must have been at that age, a farm boy beginning to play high school sports. Even then, when I was a teenager and he had long since survived those two attacks of rheumatic fever, he now and then liked to run. He would suddenly begin to skip along, and sometimes make of it a jogging gait. He did this in railroad stations between trains when we were on the way to see the relatives in New Jersey, or to visit my mother's Uncle Will and Aunt Cordia in Mechanicville, New York. More occasionally he would suddenly erupt into a short sprint. "Let's run," he would say, and we did. It was the most impulsive thing I ever saw him do in his otherwise exceedingly ordered life. Sometimes the running became more than a spontaneous quickening of pace. Now and again he would say, "Let's race." And we did. And he always won when he ran his best—until that day on the sidewalk in front our house when I was fourteen.

We were walking home in early autumn, past Doc Woodworth's old place and toward Lura's house next door, when my father said, "Come on, Dave, let's race. I'll beat you." And we ran all-out. I ran with adolescent enthusiasm, and my father ran with a suddenly gathered determination to prove he could do something he once could. In his day, when he had beaten the favored runner from Lambertville in the half-mile to crown little Clinton High with a moment of glory, it would have been no contest. I was not fast afoot and would have been no match for him.

We broke into a sprint together. He tore straight down the sidewalk with remarkable quickness for a man past his mid-forties. I took a step to the left to give us both room to maneuver, and claimed the grass for my lane. I felt a sudden burst of energy and delight, and for the first time, a sense that I might win. Then just as suddenly, he fell, hard and painfully. The walnut tree between the sidewalk and the road had sent its roots beneath the cement walk and raised and cracked it. We had all walked over or around the spot a thousand times, but now it came up to defeat my father. He didn't stumble, he didn't stagger, he just fell—abruptly and hard. I realized something had happened and I broke stride. By the time I pulled up and went back to see how he was, he was trying, slowly, to get up.

"I've hurt myself," he said, feeling each hand with the other. "I've hurt myself."

"Are you all right?" I asked anxiously. Obviously he was not altogether all right. He had just announced that he was hurt. But I asked it anyway.

"I've hurt myself, Boy," he said, standing up now. "I've hurt my hand." He had taken the full-tilt fall smack on his hands, and that may have saved him from serious injury. "I've hurt my hand," he said, favoring the right one. "I hope I haven't broken anything."

I felt helpless to do anything. He was up on his feet with no apparent injury, except for possible bruises, save for his hand. It hurt him now as we started for the house.

"I can't outrace you anymore," he said. There was no sense of my having won, of his being defeated by me. We had just begun to run when he fell. If I was not sure then I am certain now that his meaning was that he had failed. It would have been easy to blame the treacherous sidewalk or to demand a more decent running condition. But he didn't. All he said was, "I can't outrace you anymore."

Why had he tried? The artists always have it best, and Tennessee Williams gets it right when he has Brick Pollitt explain to his niece why he had tried to jump the high hurdles on the high school track, and succeeded only in hurting his ankle. "Because," he says to her when she asks why, "people like to do what they used to do, even after they've stopped being able to do it."

People in Merom had quickly learned that I was adopted. We were always amused, however, when someone at the Institute for a meeting or a conference tried to establish a physical resemblance between my parents and me. As I was growing up, it was not illogical to suggest that I resembled my mother more because of the shape and bone structure of our faces. "I think he looks more like you, Carol," someone would say, and my mother would laugh with delight and say, "Oh, isn't that nice." She was a half foot shorter than my father, who was only five feet eight, and eventually I outgrew them both by so much that the difference became the distinguishing feature among us.

As it was our life and work together at home, so it was our life and work together at Merom Institute. Perhaps some of the responsibilities laid upon me felt like impositions; they must have for a boy growing up. The overwhelming thing I felt, however, was inclusion and importance and self-esteem. My father would commandeer me to help him teach a new game or folk dance to a fresh group of campers on Sunday night in the gym. He learned them from books or records or at the Christmas Country Dance School at Berea College in Kentucky, which we often enjoyed, and I learned them from him. He believed in demonstrating a new step or figure, in showing people how it was supposed to be. Often my mother was his partner, and sometimes I was. "I need you, Davey Boy," he would say. "You've got to help me or I'm licked."

My father took it for granted that I would learn to work, and turned me over to Herald Mahan, the caretaker at the Institute who presided over the buildings and grounds. Herald was known about town as the Beetle. About my father's age, perhaps a year or two older, he was a man of patient disposition and surprising versatility. People joked about the way he took his time, but following him around for a day or two could wear you out. He knew enough about plumbing, carpentry, electricity, motors, and general maintenance to fix whatever broke and start whatever stopped. He was shrewd; nobody ever out-bargained the Beetle. Every day he milked the cow he kept at pasture a mile from his little house on the campus.

The buildings clustered at the crest of a gentle hill that rose from the east, west, and north sides of the campus. Cement block "cabins" bearing the names of leading churchmen from the Congregational-Christian tradition housed campers and conferees. One was named for Washington Gladden, who was, my father told me one day as we walked past, a Congregational minister from Ohio active in the "social gospel" movement. The main building, College Hall, dated from the beginning of old Union Christian College. Its four and a half brick stories rose to a height of a hundred and twenty-five feet; its wooden cupola, reached by one of only three circular wooden staircases in Indiana, was visible for miles on both the Indiana and Illinois sides of the Wabash. A newer brick building included a gymnasium and a chapel, a combination immensely pleasing both practically and symbolically to my father.

The gym needed cleaning daily during its constant summer use, as did the large dining room in a building named for Arthur Erastus Holt, who helped conceive and give birth to Merom Institute. Between my father's office and the kitchen, where I often ate, the dining room was dominated by a mural covering the entire wall. Painted by a conscientious objector housed at Merom Institute during World War II, it depicted want and suffering in a world of greed and war. I swept the floor day after day under the gaze of the mural's huge central figure: a farmer plucking corn from a stalk, representing hope and peace, beneath which Holt's words declared that "A world based on force and hate will destroy itself." Years later the dining room would be named for my parents. Also a room in College Hall would be designated the "Alan Jones Library."

So I swept floors and carried out garbage and ran errands, and when I was eleven or twelve, supervised by my new mentor, I began to mow the grass. Always I mowed the grass. I had no more comprehension of how a power mower worked than I did of how a garden tractor ran; I only knew that if it ran I could cut the grass. We had then an old reel-type mower which threatened continually to cut unevenly, and which often threw the chain which provided propulsion from its sprocket. Whenever that happened I sought the Beetle.

As he worked on a piece of machinery or tried to repair a faulty fixture, Herald would pause to scratch his head, his other hand resting on his hip and now holding the cap he always wore to crown his gray or tan gabardine work clothes—as easily recognizable in Merom as a policeman's uniform in a city. He would reflect for a moment, and then say in a puzzled yet searching tone, "I don't understand all I know about it." There was no point in trying to explain any of it to me. Still he wanted me to be part of his work, and so he said, "I don't understand all I know about it." This was chatter, I felt, friendly, but chatter nonetheless. Years later, I began to realize the Beetle's insight: knowledge does not guarantee understanding.

The grass did not stop at the edge of the lawns about the buildings. The campus spread out across the rest of the twenty-seven acres, and was mowed with tractor and sickle. By about fourteen I began to take it over, and all through high school I alternated following the mower across the lawns and riding the tractor out on the campus. When we arrived, Merom Institute owned an old Massey Harris, but it soon gave way to an International Harvester Cub. On this I spent hours, day after day, week after week, through the summer months. They might have been boring; they were among the best hours of my life. On that tractor, chugging and clattering along, I had to watch carefully what I did, especially to avoid harming small trees my father had planted and to be sure I didn't turn over on some tricky slopes. One learns immediately that all this is mechanical; the mind and the imagination are free to roam. Nancy has always kidded me about talking to myself, and I must have begun it during those long hours alone that were never lonely under an Indiana sun, always in view of those fabled Hoosier sycamores on the banks of the Wabash. I mowed one spot behind our house at the top of the bluff, which my father made into a place of worship, and where nature mysticism crept into the Christian presence celebrated after supper and before an evening of folk dancing in the gym.

Always I depended on the Beetle. The nemesis of mowing with the old-fashioned sickle bar, which we eventually replaced with a rotary mower, was that one of the teeth in the bar could work loose and be lost, or occasionally break against a rock or a large tree. The mowing would now become uneven, and I had to stop for repairs. More commonly the point of one of the serrated sections of the blade would break off, with an even more pronounced consequence of patches and streaks of uncut grass. Always I was helpless to do anything but raise the bar and head in to find the Beetle. If I had lost a tooth from the bar I searched until I found it and then presented it to him for replacing. That was simple—for the Beetle. Perhaps I could have done it, but I never did. If one of the blade points broke, Herald replaced the entire blade. He kept three or four on hand, and regularly took broken ones down to a blacksmith shop with a hand-fired forge. Shug Rusk was our village smithy and he had the arms to prove it. So far as I ever knew, the only thing Shug, a widower, did for diversion from his work was to drive to Sullivan every Wednesday night for the movie at the Lyric Theatre. The custom was to congregate at the county seat on Saturday, when the week's work was done and folks could anticipate a Sabbath relatively free from toil. Shug always went on Wednesday, because that was bank night and he went for the drawing. Every week he went. I don't believe he ever won, but he never failed to go. Such was the faith of a small-town blacksmith whom time and technology had overtaken, but in whom hope never died.

The Beetle, meanwhile, plied his multiple skills up at the Institute, walking about smoking terrible-smelling cigars (stogies measured time and distance; Cincinnati, for example, was about "two cigars away"), muttering now and then that "this would be a good job if it wasn't for these damned kids," and, more reflectively, that "I don't understand all I know about it." And all the time of growing up from fourteen on, I rode the tractor on the campus and along the bluff, alone with dream and imagination, the world shut out by the clatter of the mower.

My father was by practice and perhaps by temperament, though I have never been sure in just what proportion, given to diplomacy rather than confrontation. He had always told me what to do around the house and in the garden, and that seemed normal enough. As I grew older, he could tell me what he wanted done at the Institute in ways he never felt free to do with anyone else. He would coax rather than confront, persuade rather than pressure. Except with me. But he was honest about it. He often told me, "Look, Son, I can push you around the way I can't anybody else. You can take it. You know I love you; it's just that sometimes I have to have something done, and I can't make Herald do it. I have to let him work around to things his own way. He's wonderful at staying on the job and taking responsibility for the place, and I feel confident in leaving him in charge when we all have to be away. But there are times when something needs immediate attention, and you're the only one I can lean on." There was no arrogance in it; there was rather helplessness, and a hint of desperation. If a floor needed sweeping, or the grass cutting, or some shrubbery trimming, or some furniture moving, and he grew panicky that it wouldn't be done in time, he bossed me to it. I could hear his voice as I went about the task, never doubting his earnestness, and actually feeling what I think he wanted me to feel: that he was singling me out not only for work but for praise. Later, while I was in college, he managed to raise the money for a swimming pool, and I became the lifeguard and pool attendant. Herald ran the machine that controlled the water intake and outflow, but I kept the pool clean. My father was especially sensitive to its appearance. He was downright touchy. Whenever a new group was scheduled to arrive or some special guest was due to appear, and the swimming pool was not free from debris with its bottom freshly brushed, he would send me out there, sometimes peremptorily, to clean it up. Afterwards, he always said again that he knew I understood that he could "push me around." And I did.

What growing up and working at Merom Institute gave me was what everyone needs and what is sorely lacking in modern life: a sense of work that matters. Because I was never on my own but always part of a family effort, and because it was clear that the things I did were important to Merom Institute, and because I had an increasing sense of the significance of the institution itself, I knew I was helping to do something worthwhile. My father used to say to me that Paul Tillich had it right in insisting that people want to be more than a part of a part; they want to be part of a whole. That is how I felt there, and largely because of the way he brought me along. My mother felt the same way, but her life was not essentially different than it had been in earlier parishes. Then I had been the minister's son, first a baby and then a small child, expected to behave in public. Here I was, as my father often said, "part of the family team." He believed it, and I came to feel it. If we live between memory and hope, as people of faith attest, then my Merom experience has proved inexhaustible. I put my hands in clean dirt, helped things grow, picked and dug them when they were ripe, and carried out the garbage afterwards, all the while keeping the grass cut. I did that literally, and it became a metaphor.

I had gone to church since I was old enough to be taken, but not until Merom did I really hear my father preach. He was fond of recalling that Reinhold Niebuhr used to say that a sermon ought always to be a bit "in the rough." You shouldn't be absolutely certain of everything you would say too far ahead of time. He shied away from writing a manuscript, but worked hard at sermon preparation. One of my enduring images of him is at his desk in his study, either bent over writing or leaning back in his chair reading, usually wearing his green visor.

Later he taught himself to type and installed a portable typewriter table at the left side of his desk, and an old oak revolving bookcase to his right. There he is in my memory, at his desk in his green visor, typewriter to the left and bookcase to the right, working away. He loved being out in his garden and he loved being at his desk.

His great theme was the sovereignty of God. He would say to his Merom congregation again and again that "God is God." I think he absorbed this emphasis during his year in Germany at the University of Halle. For all his admiration of Harry Emerson Fosdick, I do not think he derived this insistence from him, or from American liberal theology generally.

He quoted Niebuhr and gave me Fosdick's books and remembered with affection Henry Sloane Coffin, but he spoke now more often of someone else who loomed larger and larger in his ministry. John Coleman Bennett had been a young tutor at Union when my father had been a student there in the late nineteen-twenties, and I would hear him say of Bennett that "he was keen even then." His earlier heroes would always remain special, but "we look to John for leadership," I heard him say more than once. "He's helpful."

My father sometimes went on preaching missions in Indiana or Illinois which took him away from home for a week at a time. On Sunday after he conducted the regular service in the chapel and we ate a hasty lunch, he would drive the three of us to Terre Haute where he caught a train. My mother drove us home and then back to meet him at the train the following Saturday. This happened four consecutive weeks one winter. On one of the Sundays we started back toward Merom from the station, I saw a billboard advertisement for the Ray Milland movie "It Happens Every Spring" and asked my mother to take me. I think she enjoyed that film about a college chemistry professor whose secret desire to be a big league pitcher comes true, and it remains one of my favorites, in part because she took me to see it.

During those weeks my mother took over and made decisions my father ordinarily made. She was in charge. She said the blessing before a meal and saw that one of us tended the furnace. Evenings we often played cards. Earlier she had entertained me with Authors and Old Maid. Now we played Rook, and sometimes Millie Mahan came over for Canasta in front of the fireplace in our living room. My mother had always been there to comfort me and cheer me on. She had, as Nancy would put it, "loved me into being." Now with him away, in one of my father's familiar expressions, she "called the shots."

When my Sunday School class dwindled to my teacher, the Beetle's wife Millie, and me, I was adopted by the men of the church. It was one of the good fortunes of my life. Sunday after Sunday, among fathers and grandfathers, I watched and listened and learned, a boy among the men. Gault Pleasant, a Clark University Ph. D. and former professor in old Union Christian College, and Adam French, a local farmer, taught the class and introduced me to the Socratic method. They prepared rigorously but did not lecture. Each was exceptionally intelligent and each knew, Gault from his own teaching experience and Adam from his instinct, that the irreducible necessity of fine teaching is to ask a good question. That is how each of them always opened the class, and those men who came Sunday after Sunday to sit around a large table in the small dining room in Holt Hall—a carpenter, the postmaster, a disabled farmer, a construction worker—said what they felt and thought and believed and wondered about. Some wore coats and ties and some didn't, and some smoked as they talked and listened and talked back, and Gault Pleasant and Adam French let them go at it without constraint, always relating the thing at hand to the theme or the text for the morning. I learned about teaching and learning in that Sunday School class, and I learned from those men, one and sometimes two generations older than I, that something of value can never really be a digression, nor irrelevant to Christian faith.

The whole was more than helping the Beetle. It was becoming part of the life lived at Merom Institute by the boys and girls and men and women who came there for a week in the summer. The Christian Church proclaims a universalism ordinarily belied in its local parish life, where pettiness reigns and strife abounds. Summer church conferences brought together people from different congregations, counties, and states. Most were denominational; still they became gathered communities. There emerged special friendships from those days and weeks, and what can only be called fellowship. Given a natural interest of boys in girls and girls in boys—the long curving walk from College Hall down to the corner of the campus across from our house was dubbed "lovers' lane"—some of the ministers worried about the boys and girls pairing off, but my father was very practical about it. "If we want our Protestant young people to marry other Protestant young people," he said to me, "then we'd better give them a chance to get acquainted." He saw nothing wrong with holding hands on the walk, but drew the line at that, as I do here.

In the late nineteen forties and fifties my mother and father welcomed thousands of people to Merom Institute, and they were not all Congregationalists. Presbyterians, Methodists, and many others came to the campus. The Evangelical and Reformed Church, which would shortly join with the Congregational and Christian Churches to form the United Church of Christ, was an increasing presence. This ecumenical spirit, always evident in my mother and father, was fundamental to him, and it extended to non-church groups. After he died, I found his response for a fiftieth-anniversary publication of his Rutgers class of 1926. He wrote:

"Possibly my greatest satisfaction in seventeen years as Director of Merom Institute was in cooperating with a wide variety of character-building agencies—Protestant churches of a dozen different denominations, Soil Conservation, Extension Service, Camp Fire Girls, Boy Scouts, Girl Scouts, YM and YW, mental health organizations, etc. in the fun of playing together and working to 'beat the devil' to make this a better world." He had said it earlier and more concisely for the *Terre Haute Tribune*: "We seek to cooperate with all groups desiring that man's total life be more abundant."

There was more. Merom Institute became a world in miniature. To it came Negroes from different sections of the United States, usually as leaders and resource people for conferences. These were the first American Negroes many of the young people had seen. My father was not a crusader, but he was delighted to welcome the Fisk Jubilee Singers to the campus, and in 1948, when the Chautauqua was revived at Merom Bluff, a troop of singers and dancers from Harlem was housed and fed there. They were exotic in Merom; it seemed quite natural that they should stay at Merom Institute. There were Africans, including

Ndabaningi Sithole, who would emerge as one of the black nationalist leaders in Rhodesia as that country became Zimbabwe. We had all sung "In Christ There is no East or West," but it was largely an abstraction until white, often rural, midwestern Protestant Americans met black Americans and Africans.

American Indians appeared, offering many of us our first chance to realize how tragically stereotyped the movies made them. Now and then a rabbi attended a conference, providing yet another exposure most had lacked. My father, publicly open to anyone and everyone, privately grumbled about what he regarded as the unnecessary trouble orthodox rabbinic guests caused the kitchen staff. Christians from Hawaii, the Philippines, and China came to Merom. Half a dozen years after the end of World War II a Japanese Christian spent some summer weeks at Merom Institute. We washed dishes together at my mother's sink. This was a wider world. What would later become clearer and more fully magnified was already apparent in that green and pleasant place on the banks of the Wabash.

The World Council of Churches, organized in 1948 in Amsterdam, met in 1954 at the First Methodist Church in Evanston, Illinois, Chicago's nearest northern neighbor. It was natural for my father to want to attend; the World Council fused his ecumenical and cosmopolitan impulses. It was also convenient; Merom was but two hundred miles directly south of Chicago. My mother and I went with him because he wanted us to. We stayed in Wilmette with one of his seminary friends. He took in the World Council and my mother and I went to Comiskey Park. On a June Sunday, because she knew I wanted to, we went down to see the White Sox play the Tigers a double-header.

Baseball and death are the great equalizers, and I talked that day with a perfect stranger, middle-aged and middle-sized, who sat beside me away from my mother. She knew next to nothing of the game, and cared as little for it. She was making me happy. My new neighbor would not be still. His great theme, which he brooded over through the afternoon, was the mystery of Fred Hatfield's hitting.

"That Fred Hatfield," he would say of one of the best-fielding third basemen in the American League, "I'll bet he hits .600 against the White Sox. I <u>do</u> not understand it. I do <u>not</u>." And indeed Hatfield hit safely throughout the afternoon as we watched and the Chicagoan talked. He looked too scrawny to be a major league ball player, but the Detroit third baseman made disgruntled believers of White Sox fans, and my companion could only say again and again, "I <u>do</u> not understand it, I do <u>not</u>." I doubt that Hatfield did.

To be alive for me that day was to see Al Kaline. He was nineteen years old and in his first full season with Detroit, the year before he would win his only batting title and do it as the youngest man ever to record such an achievement. He beat Tyrus Raymond Cobb, the greatest Tiger of them all, to that distinction by one day on the birthday calendar. There he was before me, a fellow teenager, a skinny kid in the Tiger outfield wearing the promise of future greatness. They listed him at 170 pounds, but I doubt if he weighed more than 150 that year. His uniform hung on him; the major league teams had not yet gone to more mod cuts. Even the oversized baseball suit could not conceal the great natural gifts he brought to the game. He did everything as a baseball player should. He stood up at the plate and stroked the ball cleanly and surely. He ran the bases with good speed and more importantly with an obvious intelligence. And he played right field like a veteran, possessed of that certain instinct all great outfielders have for getting off with the crack of the bat in the right direction to make a play. Even then, on that day in June when he was yet a skinny teenager, he showed that he could become the American League's finest throwing right fielder. He had it all, and he was not yet twenty years old. I was enthralled, and have been a Tiger fan since.

Kaline tripled "up the alley" in right center field his first time up against Virgil "Fire" Trucks, running as gracefully as he had swung the bat. He got five hits that day that I remember, and I have not checked the record. That would profane the sacred. That day belongs to memory and myth and my mother. She went with me not for baseball and not for Kaline and not for herself and not even to escape from the World Council of Churches. She went to make me happy. And on that day I was, as Dylan Thomas wrote, as "happy as the grass was green."

A visual memory of my father in his prime as the Director of Merom Institute remains vivid, and gathers the aspects of his character and personality. He has come out of the dining room and is wearing summer slacks and a short-sleeved shirt open at the neck. He looks directly ahead and raises his right hand in both a wave and a blessing. His look is firm—neither stern nor jolly. He knows who he is and where he going. He knows the meaning of his life and work. The determined child in the picture of me behind the garden tractor is here the fulfilled man. He looks peaceful and content and purposeful. A picture taken just after I graduated from high school shows my father, my mother, and me on the front porch of our house. Here he smiles broadly and my mother sweetly, and we are a happy family. But my mental picture of him coming down the walk from Holt Hall, leaving his office behind for the day, hand raised in benediction, is the right remembrance of him as the Director of Merom Institute.

He wanted the Institute to serve the town as well as the denomination and the wider church and world. Fun and fellowship and good will were meant for those at home as well as those who came from up and down the Wabash Valley and from around the world. The high-school softball team practiced and played home games on the northwest corner of the campus. The basketball team practiced in the Institute gym, which was also available on winter evenings to anyone who wanted to play there. He was sure that such use of the facility was justified by its character-building potential, and at the very least gave some kids a place to play who might otherwise get into trouble. There were square dances and Halloween parties in the gym, and roller skating until the floor was so damaged it had to be replaced and skating abandoned. There were dinners in Holt Hall, where the annual high school athletic award banquet was held and high school alumni gathered yearly. Downstairs was a community laundry used heavily by local people.

He used say that because I went to school there, I was our most important connection with the town. He was too modest. Years later when I was, from time to time, back for a visit, unfailingly the first thing anyone asked was, "How's your mom and dad?" It was a confirmation of their life and work in Merom. Once LaDonna Beard, a girl with whom I had gone to school and who had worked in the kitchen at the Institute, asked about them and then said of my father, "He shaped a lot of us."

A radical egalitarianism pervaded that little town on the banks of the Wabash River. To be sure, we were religiously, ethnically, and racially homogeneous—except for the old Negro lady who lived for a time with her niece or granddaughter just off the main street near the center of town. Racial and ethnic prejudice was apparent, as it often is in the absence of those against whom it is directed. But among ourselves one thing was plain: nobody was better than anybody else, nobody. Neither age nor occupation mattered. It was all right to be better <u>at</u> something: playing basketball or the piano, cooking, fixing whatever broke down, gardening. It was forbidden to affect <u>being</u> better.

Generational segregation was unknown. Everybody knew everybody else, just as everybody knew every house and building in town. People from Fort Wayne or Evansville or Indianapolis who came to the Institute remarked on this, as I called by name everyone I saw on the sidewalk or passing in the street. This was not the stultifying conformity of Sinclair Lewis's Gopher Prairie: it was community and it knew no age. Pete Huff, the grandfather of my classmate Darrell Wesner, used to say to me, "Go home and tell your mom and dad that we'll take you to raise." Young and old and everyone in between was somebody. Nearly everyone in town had been born there. Here we were, out from New England and my parents products of New Jersey. Merom adopted me, and that is surely why I claimed it so affectionately.

Any small town finds its focus in a school, and here one was aware of temporary segregation according to age, but only here. Otherwise age did not matter; people did. Olan Vickrey once told me that "nobody ever starved in Merom." At the post office or the drug store, you could see why. Some people drank too much and we had our requisite town drunk, a man known universally as a hard and dependable worker when he was sober. Boys fought as they grew up and girls became pregnant. Families took issue with other families. Withal community prevailed.

A boy found the drug store more appealing than the post office. The only thing you could buy at the post office was a stamp or a money order. At the drug store a boy met up with his friends and palled around with older fellows and men and women. Inside on a stool at the counter or in a booth, or outside leaning against the wall or lounging on the sidewalk, camaraderie was as undifferentiated as it is in the bleachers at a ball game. Affairs of state and local lamentations dwelt side by side in conversation that was equally inclusive and opinionated. During the basketball season the team and its fortunes got top billing over gossip and racy stories.

Proprietorship changed from time to time, but the drug store directly across the street from the school remained as the unofficial civic center of Merom. It is arguable that the men and women who operated it made the most significant contribution to Merom pride and good will. Students spilled out of school and scrambled across the street at noon and after school because it was the thing to do, and because there was something special about a soda-fountain drink. In a town dotted with tiny churches, people of good will but divergent religious persuasion needed some place to gather and enter upon fellowship of heart and spirit. In Merom, that place was the drug store. I wonder whether any other institution in American life has matched it for such function.

Babe and Irene Thompson took it over, and Babe ran the ferry after I went away to college, but as I grew up they lived across the road from the northeast corner of the campus, from where the Babe commuted to a job in Terre Haute. They had six children, the oldest known as Rat and the youngest named for me.

"David," Babe would say, "it takes all kinds to make a world." Then thinking on it, he would add, "Well, it doesn't take 'em, but we've got 'em anyway." Or "David, it's a wide, wide world. She's not too long, but she sure is wide."

He sometimes came across the road to the campus to play ball with his children and Hukey Rinard and me. He was a powerful man, at least six feet tall and very muscular and strong, but he was careful not to hurt us. When I announced to him a longing to be a big-leaguer, he said sympathetically, "David, you're not hardly heavy enough."

Babe was a biblical literalist who would not have understood the meaning of myth as students of religion use the term. It was all quite simple and direct. Here is how it happened and this is what is promised still to come. It is so written. Years later he would say to me abruptly when Nancy and I stopped by, "David, I don't hardly see how He can wait much longer." We knew he spoke of Christ's second coming, an event he expected as surely as his own earthly demise. "The way things are now, getting to be more like Sodom and Gomorrah every day, I just don't see how He can wait."

I went to school in Merom from fifth grade through high school. Now we debate the optimum number of students a teacher should have in a class; there was no issue for us. My high school graduating class boasted nineteen people. We knew the teachers cared about us, though we knew they also despaired at times of teaching us much. The offerings were, predictably, limited. I learned no Latin and no modern foreign languages and did not even have a chance to take English my senior year. I was taught physics and chemistry by a math teacher, and biology by a short-term principal who had never had the subject. But emotionally and psychically and socially we waxed rather than waned.

The radical egalitarianism so present in the town saturated the school. Sizes and abilities differed, but nobody was better than anybody else. A claim to moral superiority was inadmissible; rank by status was altogether unbelievable. Tracking was unknown, and there were no accelerated classes. Everyone was in it together. Students quickly ranked themselves according to ability and effort. That was as it should be. But there was no trading on superior performance. One wore it at school and left it there. The veneration of the average American was, in such an atmosphere, a distinct possibility. Just as compelling was the undeniable implication that all were equal and none were more equal than others.

The school, which became township-consolidated at the high-school level in 1950, was the center of the community and its life. Teachers were loved and respected, and sometimes legendary. There was an implicit partnership between school and home and between school and church. This was Protestant country, before the Bible-reading and school-prayer decisions of the Supreme Court in the early 1960's, and nobody worried about violating the Constitutional separation of church and state. Rat Thompson was so good at reproducing gospel songs he had learned in the Assembly of God church that teachers sometimes gave way to popular student demand to have him sing one in class. His standard was "This World is Not My Home"; he also favored "Power in the Blood." We called a teacher, also the coach and later to be the principal, by his first name. Only the other teachers called him Mr. Owens. He was Charlie to us.

Sports mattered. Basketball was played in Connecticut; to come into Indiana basketball is to enter upon something which vastly transcends a game. In southern Indiana basketball was of life's very meaning. It just <u>was</u>. With certain understood exceptions, it was expected that one would play. Everyone knew that some were better than others: bigger, stronger, faster, more naturally gifted. But one played. It was rather like one's patriotic duty, to fight for one's country in time of war. As the army recognized deficiencies which disqualified one from active duty, so the Indiana ethic knew that not everyone was meant to dribble and rebound and shoot. This was only a minor distinction. Basketball was what mattered. He who did not play went to cheer and talked of little else. If school was required and if the drugstore was an occasion, basketball was our unending cause. This was the more true because few students advanced to college. High school was taken to be the end of formal education. Boys, girls, men, women, and little children all combined to form an unbroken cheering section before, during, and after games. The movie "Hoosiers" does not exaggerate.

This was all new to me, and I was no athlete. Small, light, timid, and afflicted with some congenital deficiencies of leg and foot, I was a very poor prospect. Most of all, early on I lacked a sense of calling to the game. That is the only way to put it, for if boys outgrew (if, I say; I am not sure some ever did) their zeal for the game after high school, until the season ended unhappily—as it must for everyone but the state champion—it was one's great passion. It was part fun, part achievement, part duty, part rite of passage. It takes money and equipment to play some sports, and the right climate and facilities for others, but anybody can tack a hoop up on a barn or shed or pole and scrounge up enough money to buy a ball. Everything that has been written about Hoosier Mania is an understatement, everything. It is nothing short of religion, the true faith. Into this new world I came at age nine.

I was no good and too small to be promising. I tried to play for my school in the fifth grade and got nowhere. I didn't bother in the sixth. The following year I logged time on the "second team," and in the eighth grade we won the county championship. I had sense enough to know that I was the weakest member of that team. At five feet four and less than a hundred pounds I decided not to try out as a high-school freshman. Charlie Owens, our first-name teacher and at that time the coach, spoke to me one day at school three weeks into practice.

"Why don't you come on out," he said. "I know you're discouraged because you're too small, but I think you're going to grow someday because you've got such big feet."

It was a word in season. My feet were as flat as they were long, and I would eventually wear a size twelve shoe and make a prophet of Charlie by topping six feet. He would see me after school during the off season, or in the summer months, and demand, "Why aren't you up there in the gym firing away at the baskets?" There was never anything to do but head for the gym. Realizing my natural limitations, I determined to become a good shot. This was when the game of basketball was still played on or close to the floor, and skill in shooting could compensate for lack of speed or size or leaping ability far more than now. I was a coachable kid—if you lack talent you may be more coachable than if you have it—who learned to shoot a basketball. But I never became the ballplayer my teammates were.

My mother little understood basketball, and the game was changing rapidly from the one my father had played when he was in high school and college. Sometimes she attended games, and he nearly always did, as a parent shows up at school to see his child in a play or a class program. He seldom said anything, but he was there. Always the Puritan and jealous of time, he would take along something to read, often a recent issue of *The Christian Century*, and during a timeout, and especially at halftime, he read. A large cohort of men, fathers of boys on the team and other well-wishers, regularly headed for the men's rest room at the half to smoke. It was as much a ritual as an addiction. At the buzzer signaling the half, they would rise from their seats in the bleachers and make their customary way to the smoker. My father remained where he sat and turned to *The Christian Century*. Men going by on their way to smoke would speak and he would respond; each understood the purpose of the other. I have often wondered whether anyone else in the history of Indiana high school basketball read *The Christian Century* at a game.

My mother cared that I ate properly and had plenty of sleep, and did not understand the peculiar challenges the game presented to me. I knew I needed to be more aggressive, but nothing in my life at home encouraged this. My father was a stickler for fair play, and my mother did not think it appropriate for bodies to collide and tangle on the floor. Even then basketball was far from a non-contact sport, even at the high-school level. There was plenty of contact; the more aggressive players ran into other people and banged against the floor with equal enthusiasm and frequency. My mother was quite persuaded that such brutality was not for me, yet she managed to recognize that speed and quickness were important to the game, and that body contact and fouls could not altogether be avoided. We talked one day in our kitchen when I was a high school junior and she resolved it.

"I like the way you play with restraint," she said, "and yet with abandon."

It was perfect. If nobody else in the state of Indiana read *The Christian Century* at high school basketball games, nobody else could have conceived such a way to estimate a player's style, much less have said it so. That was my mother, precisely and predictably. In truth, I was more restrained than abandoned.

My father had been a more aggressive athlete than I. Growing up among brothers doubtless helped make him so. He told me that aggressive play in basketball had given him an advantage over bigger opponents. Whether his illnesses changed him or whether his understanding of the Christian life caused him to adopt a gentle and kindly stance toward other people, he was ambivalent toward me as I tried to play ball. One should compete in a friendly way; one should play cleanly and be a good sport. On the other hand, he told me I was not aggressive enough, and he was right. It was a great weakness in my play. Everybody knew it, and most of all myself. Yet everything in his example led me away from toughness and that killer instinct so celebrated in sports.

The tension in this ambivalence was revealed perfectly in a softball game my senior year in high school. We knew we had the best team in the county, and that, unless we beat ourselves, we would win the county championship. We did. Dean

Ridge was too fast for any other team to hit, his brothers Jerome and Gary were uncompromising competitors, Darrell Wesner was a fine athlete, and the rest of us filled in, I at second base. All we had to do was play. In a home game on the Merom Institute campus, I was on first base as our leadoff hitter, and the batter hit a ground ball to the left side of the infield. It was a picture-book double-play ball if fielded and handled cleanly. The shortstop scooped it up and threw over to the second baseman for the force out on me. The task of the base runner in such a case is plain: take out, if he can, the second baseman so that he cannot complete the double play. In what may have been the most aggressive play I had ever made, I did precisely that, sliding into him and knocking him completely off balance so that he fell on top of me. He held the ball for the force out, but had no chance for the double play. I took his feet out from under him, he came down and I got up, and everybody on our team, led by the coach, cheered my effort. It was as much because I had done it, out of character, as that it helped the team. I made that play according to the book. The team loved it.

My father saw the game and waited for me afterward so that we could walk home together. We had won, and I felt good about my play at second. Surely he would commend me for <u>this</u>, having properly pointed out more than once that I held back too much and too often. He was dismayed, and lectured me less sternly than sorrowfully on the merits of good sportsmanship and clean play. I tried to explain that I <u>had</u> been a good sport and that it was a perfectly clean play. He would have none of it. It would not do to knock somebody down. Vainly did I try to expound the dynamics of the game, even as I remembered his stories of running into bigger opponents in basketball. None of us wore spikes; we all wore tennis shoes. There was no sharpened metal to hurt anyone. There were no hard feelings. The other second baseman and I knew each other. I had done what he would have done. But for my father, I had done a bad thing, and he hoped I would never repeat it.

Early in the basketball season I made him happy by stopping to help up a fallen opponent. Our coach, by then Charlie's successor, was furious, and told me that the only reason he didn't pull me out of the game was that only seconds remained to be played when I did it. "Don't ever give an opponent an advantage," he preached to me at game's end, right there at the edge of the court before we even made it into the locker room. "Don't do that. If he falls down, go around him and keep going. That gives us the advantage. If the score had been tight you might have cost us the game." I don't know whether I would have stopped to pick him up if anything had been at stake. We were ahead by nearly twenty points in the final minute of play. My father loved it, thought it decent and Christian, and made a point of saying that it pleased him especially because of the rough stuff around second base back during the softball season.

He rarely praised me for anything I did in sport. Once, when he was "hitting them out" to me, I went back for a soft liner as an infielder should, sprinting away from the batter, and took the ball in my glove, stretched as far as I could. At that he said, "You're good, Dave." That was the only time. When the coach posted the statistics after the softball season my junior year, I eagerly told him I had led the team in batting. He made no response; my mother thought it was a splendid achievement. After I scored eighteen points in the first half of a basketball game in my senior year, a friend told me that another man jabbed my father and asked, "What do you think of that, Alan?" and he said nothing. He was there, he saw it, but he did not commend me. Again, my mother thought it was wonderful. I was less bothered than puzzled by him. Looking back, and hearing others comment, it seems stranger than it felt then. It had nothing to do with rejection; I felt completely secure in our family. He must have been torn between parental pride and some Christian compulsion to avoid the appearance of pride. Perhaps he sought to inspire me with humility: play your best but take it all in stride and let someone else claim the credit and glean the glory. It's clear, Son, that you are not aggressive enough for your own good as ballplayer, but we all know that Jesus' humility was perfect. Keep your head and be a good sport.

In the 1950s every small school in Indiana wanted to claim a state sectional basketball championship, of which there were then sixty-four. Indiana high schools were not then divided into different classifications according to enrollment. Every team, from schools large and small, competed in the same state tournament. The movie "Hoosiers" was based on the "Milan miracle" of 1954, when the Milan team, representing a school of one hundred and fifty students, implausibly won the state championship by beating perennially powerful and sometime state champion Muncie Central. Realistically people throughout the state knew just how improbable it was, and how unlikely anyone could do it again. But it was possible to imagine a small school could get over the first hurdle in the state tournament and win the coveted sectional. In our case it included all the teams in Sullivan County. As we had won the country tournament as eighth-graders, perhaps inspired by Milan we captured the state sectional tournament as high school seniors in 1955. It was a glorious moment for Gill Township High School's seventy-five students and everyone in the township. The dream of advancing further died in the first game of the state regional tournament.

My father never went as far as did Francis Cardinal Spellman's, who advised his son always to associate with people smarter than himself, which, he told him, should not be difficult. There was, however, a strange and uncertain tension between encouragement and blunt criticism intended to deflect any hint of presumption. What remains unclear is whether such reminders of my mortality and finitude were really aimed at me or represented some projection of himself upon me. He made this plain by insisting that I attend summer school at Indiana State Teachers College, now Indiana State University, in Terre Haute following my high school graduation. Merom remained on standard time and Terre Haute ran on daylight time. That meant getting up about five in the morning, which was already six in Terre Haute, to make an early morning class. It meant homework had to be done the night before.

I played on a softball team that summer, and late one afternoon was eating a snack just before heading off for a game. We played under lights in a summer league, and that lent a certain glamour to it, even as we knew we didn't quite belong on the field. Our team was made up of boys and we played against men. As I gulped down a glass of milk, my father walked behind me and asked if I had done my homework. No, I said, between gulps. You'd better get to it, he replied, you don't want to put it off until too late at night. Finishing my milk I announced that I couldn't do it just now because I had to go play ball. Just as quickly he replied that I could not expect to get by in class by "pulling it off the top of your head" at the last minute. "You can't do that," he said, "because you're not bright enough."

I didn't know then and I don't know now whether he was worried about me academically, or whether he felt constrained to reinforce a moral maxim I had heard so often: that hard work will produce some proper reward, and it is pure self-deception to think anything else will be rewarded. I did play that night, and I worked to prepare for my classes when I got home. I'm sure we lost the game because we lost nearly every one we played. I never lost the memory of what my father said.

The night I went away to college I felt ambivalent. Who has not on leaving home? I had taken courses at Indiana State during the summer, but I had commuted for that and it was in no way the same thing as pulling up and leaving to go to school four hundred miles away. I had, on my own, never imagined attending Oberlin College; my father thought it would be a good thing. When I hear and read that children and youth should make their own decisions and that parents have no business trying to tell them what to do, or tell them what's good for them, I remember that my father decided that I should go to Oberlin—if the college would have me—and that I have been grateful ever since. I did not know enough always to realize what was good for me, and he—always he and not my mother, who simply agreed with him on it—moved me in directions he thought I should go. He was not always right, but he was right about Oberlin.

I had been to the campus the previous spring and liked it and its people immediately. Those things just happen. An earlier visit to a small Midwestern college left me uninspired. Oberlin was different. There for a short weekend, I fell in love with it and have remained enthralled since. It is a special place with a special history and a special attraction, but it is not for everyone. At our twenty-fifth reunion, a classmate married to a Princeton graduate said, "Reunions at Princeton are not like this." The college has long since given up its deliberate identification with evangelical Protestantism, but the fruits of the spirit of that evangelical impulse remain part of the legacy. Generalizations always distort, but I think it is fair to say that the Oberlin tradition, even as it makes its way now into the twenty-first century, is one which not only insists on learning and labor, as the college motto proclaims, but one which energetically encourages caring— for things of mind and spirit, for the state of the world, and most of all for other people. I was uneasy about "proving myself" at Oberlin, but I wanted to go. I had no idea of its meaning academically, culturally, and intellectually; I knew only that it enjoyed a good reputation. My father thought I should "go to Oberlin" and I went.

I assumed that he, or perhaps my mother, would drive me out and deliver me, as parents do. But he was unsentimental in such things; to get me to Oberlin was a logistics problem, nothing else. If someone else could do it, so much the better. Someone else did. My father came home from his office a couple of days before I was to leave and announced, "I've got a ride for you to Oberlin." Some ministers he knew who had often been to the Institute would be attending a conference at Oberlin scheduled to open a day before I needed to be there. For him it was per- fect. It never occurred to me to dissent.

"They called me up and asked if I'd like to go with them to the conference," he said. "I said no, I couldn't do that, but I had a son who needed to get there to go to college, and it would be nice if _he_ could ride along. They said that would be fine, so they'll take you with them. You've met all these fellows, and you'll just be one of the boys in the car. This really will make things simpler for Mom and me," he continued after reciting their names. "It means you'll have to reorganize your packing, but that shouldn't be hard. We'll work it out so you take a suitcase or two with what you need right away, and I'll ship the trunk," referring to a recent purchase from good old reliable Sears Roebuck to mark my educational rite of passage. "There is one thing. You'll have to leave in the middle of the night."

"What do you mean I'll have to leave in the middle of the night?"

"They want to drive all night to get there, it's about an eight-hour drive or so, and they'll pick you up over at the junction of 54 and 41. They told me to have you there at one o'clock, when they'll be coming through. It's right on their way, and they'll just take you along with them instead of me. You'll have a good time."

It all made sense from his point of view, though I felt some disappointment that it would not be a family drive to college. I knew and liked the men with whom I would be riding; that would be all right. But my father would have to deliver me to the appointed place at one o'clock in the morning and that just did not suit his schedule.

"I'm sure," he said, "that you can get one of your buddies to drive you over. Ask Jerome. He'll be glad to do it."

Of course it made sense. He had secured the ride, and because of the inconvenient time that was the end of his responsibility. It wouldn't do for my mother to take me over there at such an hour, so that left it up to a friend. The transportation itself was no problem; indeed Jerome agreed to help me out. It was that my father and mother would not be taking me.

So here we were, Jerome and I, down in our living room the night I was to leave for Oberlin, and my mother and father already in bed and asleep. I was anxious because Oberlin seemed a great unknown, even though I had come to like it so quickly on that visit the spring before. I knew it would be different, that it was supposed to be different or why bother. For years my father had been telling me that college would "open up a whole new world." I could see that it mattered to him, just as it would matter to me for my children. But I did not grasp anything of what he meant, could not comprehend the promise he held out. I knew only that I must go because it was the rankest heresy to think otherwise. I would go, and I wanted to, but I was anxious.

"Wake us up before you leave so we can say goodbye to you," he instructed me as he and my mother went upstairs to bed about ten, just after Jerome appeared.

"Yes, Dear," she said, "do wake us. Oh, we do want to tell you goodbye."

Jerome had come that early to do me a favor, though he didn't say so. He and I had been close friends from the time our family arrived in Merom. He was a year older, and in many ways played the role of a big brother. There was much in him that I admired. He grew early and I grew late, and so for years he seemed much older. He not only grew early; physically he was extraordinary, though he was only five feet seven inches and a hundred and fifty pounds. People in Merom remarked on it, and I think the whole county knew it by way of watching him play basketball. In the eighth grade during a tournament game, he threw a one-handed courtlength pass that went awry and struck a post which supported the gymnasium balcony. The velocity of the pass and the impact of the ball stunned the crowd. Guy Sparks, Jerry's father, once told me that "when God made Jerome Daugherty, He put him together better than anybody in the history of Merom." It was true. There was, I thought, almost a mystical quality about his strength. He could do things physically that no one else could. And he was absolutely fearless. He was red-headed with something of the proverbial red-headed temper, but he was never mean or ugly, only high-spirited and aggressive in sports. He also had a fine tenor voice. I took a special satisfaction in our friendship because we had come to talk "on the level," as Gary Cooper said it in the movies, with each other, and I knew there was far more to him than physical impressiveness. He relished athletic competition and plunged into it with fearless abandon, but he was morally sensitive and struggled to do the right thing. Simply to feel good was not enough.

During the past summer we had double-dated and played together on the fast-pitch softball team that was out of its league. Driving over to those games or going to pick up our dates we talked of life and death, of God and man and purpose. Did I think God could have saved Billy Wright, a seventeen-year-old killed in an auto accident, he asked me one evening on the way to Sullivan? I didn't know. Did he? Yes, he said, he did, which raised without comment from either of us another question. Now, though he knew we would not leave until about midnight, he had come over because he knew I really wanted him to and needed him to. He came. Neither of us said anything about it; he just came.

We talked quietly so we would not disturb my mother and father upstairs and, we presumed, now asleep. And we smoked. We knew they would smell it the next day but we did it anyway. I had tried it on the sly now and then, never chancing it around my parents. My father frowned on it severely, often assuring me that he had never known anyone who became a better person by taking up smoking. I didn't argue and I didn't smoke around him, or much at all. Now we smoked as we talked softly of high-school basketball teams we had played on, of championships and disappointments. We talked of girls we had dated. What would become of summer romance? We talked about the past summer at Merom Institute; he had worked there those months I was in summer school at Indiana State. We even tried to imagine the future, and of course we couldn't. So we each smoked another cigarette. You have to do something. He asked me if I felt nervous, even scared, about going off to college. He had been at Purdue for a year and knew something about it. I said yes, but I wanted to go.

"Well, Dave," he said, putting out his smoke, "maybe you'd better go up there and wake up Alan and Carol. We need to leave in a few minutes in case those guys are early."

"Yeah, I'll go up now. I hate to wake 'em up, but they did want me to. O. K. I'll be right down."

I went upstairs and down the hall and into their bedroom. They both seemed asleep in their twin beds, and then my mother stirred. I went over to my father who, as always, slept on his stomach with his head turned away from the door.

"Dad," I said softly, "Dad, I've got to leave now. It's time for Jerome and me to go."

There was nothing, and I wasn't sure he'd heard. He hadn't moved.

"Dad," I said a little louder, "I've got to go now."

This time he stirred.

"I have to go. Dad, it's time for me to leave."

He raised his head just enough to turn it toward me and then put it right back face-down on his pillow. I don't think he opened his eyes.

"May the Lord bless you, Son."

He went straight back to sleep. I walked over to my mother, now quite awake, and much more concerned to tell her boy goodbye.

"Goodbye, Mom," I said. "I'll write you."

"Oh, yes, Dear, do," she said. "And I'll write you. Here, give me a kiss."

I bent down to kiss her as she reached up and put her arms around me, and as our lips touched I could hear my father snore.

"Bye, Honey," she said. "Be a good boy and do a good job. I know you will."

"Bye, Mom," I said. "I'll try."

We were waiting when the ministers arrived, and quickly transferred my luggage. I got in with them and looked back to see Jerome wheeling around to head home on route 54, back to Merom, Indiana, on the banks of the Wabash River, where his mother and father were asleep and my mother and father were asleep and probably everybody else in town was asleep. And though I didn't think it would happen, soon I was asleep in that car making for Oberlin.

Interlude

I

Robert Frost tells us in "The Death of the Hired Man" that "Home is the place where, when you have to go there, they have to take you in." Home is given, it is not negotiable; it is there, it is not problematic. We recognize the truth of this when we say, "they are like family," or "they treat me as if I were family." What this means is taken for granted, and what it means is binding. We are bound, for better or worse, by and in and through our families. Blood, we say, is thicker than water. But adoption demonstrates that blood is a symbol.

Nowhere is this more evident than in marriage. Here a man and a woman are joined together precisely outside the bonds of biology (in our culture anyway). In rare instances when cousins marry, we feel relieved in proportion to how distant they are from immediate ties of blood. What is most intimate and what society depends on to reproduce and culturally replicate itself stands, at the point of marriage or some surrogate, apart from blood. Where we are closest and most revealed, and most vulnerable, we insist on blood's absence. Marriage is adoption.

My father was right. In marriage, two people "pick each other out." They may do it more or less suddenly, more or less wisely, more or less successfully. But they do it. Marriage is mutual adoption. That is what differentiates it from adults who adopt a child. Here, in marriage, mutually consenting adults adopt each other, for better or worse. Unless the partners to it explicitly go against the traditional vows, they promise to love each other forever. We know that many marriages do not work out and that the institution is undergoing changes charted by sociologists and anthropologists and lamented by some religionists. But the condition of marriage is one brought about not by blood but by adoption. The same funda-

95

mental meaning which characterizes parental adoption of children applies to marriage: choosing and promising which produce its givenness and thereness.

This is kinship, whether between parent and child or husband and wife, for kinship is always a choosing, an embracing, an adopting. We say, colloquially, that someone is kin to us if we sense a similarity in attitude, desire, or behavior. A marriage establishes formal kinship, and not the other way around. It is the marriage that produces the kinship between husband and wife, as it is the adoption that effects it between parents and children. We are all born of blood, but we are adopted into relationships of love and meaning.

A fundamental confusion obscures the meaning I want to establish, a confusion, I think, of recent origin. People talk of "falling in love" or of "being in love." Quite clearly if one may "fall into love" one may "fall out of love." If people are "in love" they may become "out of love." People often describe their experience and seem to understand themselves in this way. They say they would like to "fall in love" again or to "be in love" once more. We hear it said of couples that they have "fallen out of love," or that "these things happen." Such feelings are real, and they produce extraordinary responses. This is the love, embracing longing and desire and passion, poets celebrate and movies display. It just happens. Contemporary America might be described as a land of "in loveness." No one should scoff at Eros.

Such, however, is not a married kind of love, any more than an occasion of birth makes for parenthood. Married love is a choosing and a committing of one person to another, and implicitly to any others which that bond may sooner or later include. In Barbara Grizzuti Harrison's *Foreign Bodies*, a character declares that "we are not free to choose those whom we are free to love." This may be true if we mean by love something we "fall into" and correspondingly "fall out of," that love "just happens," but it is nonsense if love is known as an active commitment to another, if it is regarded as a disposition of the will. In this sense we may say that love does not hold marriage together, but rather marriage holds love together. How does one "fall out of" a commitment? How does one undo an act? Love is precisely choosing, "picking out," and thus we may say that kinship is choosing. This is the truth of adoption and it is the truth of marriage. When a marriage produces children, the same demand to choose those children to love and embrace and nurture is present.

Denis de Rougement's study of *Love in the Western World* contrasted marriage with romance and concluded that they are incompatible. They are incompatible if we mean by romance what medieval knights and ladies and modern movies mean by it: that feeling, often associated with a mystery and power not unlike that ascribed to religious experience, which sweeps over one and over which one has no control. The contemporary experience of "falling in love" is a distantly removed derivative of such romance. Control, in fact, would be utterly contrary to the overwhelming force which can "make us do things" we know better than to entertain in saner moments. That is antithetical to marriage understood as a commitment to love for better or for worse. Not by chance do the traditional marriage vows omit to ask the persons joining their lives whether they love each other, much less whether they are "in love." They are asked to promise to love. That means nothing else than an active undertaking of mind and will, which we hope will be accompanied by a willing and joyful heart. But we know that the heart comes and goes, and is, to be sure, beyond the immediate control of the will and the mind. C. S. Lewis wrote that Eros makes promises that Eros can't keep. The point is that a person pledges to keep a promise whether he always feels like or not. It is this which distinguishes us as human beings. Peter Wilson, a New Zealand anthropologist, has termed man "the promising primate."

We say that blood is thicker than water, but blood is a symbol. This is never more clear than when fathers default on child-support payments. Real kinship, always a choosing, establishes a givenness from which we cannot be separated and from which we draw strength and inspiration. In a marriage kin means not blood but a deliberately chosen bond. A marriage marvelously illustrates the meaning of adoption. In kinship there are no in-laws and no outlaws. There is only family: mothers, fathers, brothers, sisters, husbands, wives, children. When people pick each other out to marry they establish kinship: its support, its structure, its promise, its givenness. When people marry, they adopt each other.

II

The American experience is an experiment in adoption. We are a nation of adoption, by adoption, and for adoption. That is our central meaning, in its dark and bright illuminations. To say this is not to fall back upon cliche or idealism, or to insist on American innocence. It is not to pretend that everyone is welcome in America, for everyone isn't. In fact, one way to view American history is to see it, in John Higham's phrase, as a story of "strangers in the land." Recent Hispanic immigration and the prospect of considerably more of it makes many Americans nervous. We could not lately agree that Central Americans fleeing war and terror in their countries were really endangered; some, and most importantly the United States government, wanted to send such refugees back to what others saw as certain danger and possible death. New Asian immigrants have not been welcomed with universal enthusiasm, especially some of the Vietnamese boat people who have tried to settle along the Gulf of Mexico. Older Asian immigrants have also felt uneasy; Japanese Americans wondered whether our annoyance and anger over trade imbalances with Japan would turn upon them. Should we imagine that somehow these signs of unfriendliness are products only of contemporary American life, and that in the past we really were the home of the brave and the land of the free, we do well to remember Will Rogers's quip that things are not as good as they used to be, and they never were.

One need not rehearse the struggle over immigration and the anxiety over an enlarging pluralism that ran steadily through the nineteenth century, and which finally saw the enactment of a national law in 1924 aimed at preventing further dilution of an Anglo-Saxon hegemony in American culture and society. American history is in considerable measure ethnic history and minority group history. To recognize that recent historical research demonstrates deprivation and oppression in the American story does not make one a cynic. We have always been choosy about whom to let in and whom to keep out, and the central paradox of our past, the paradox of freedom and slavery, contained the anomaly of forcefully bringing to our land a large and unwilling group which was then denied the promise of American life.

To say we are a nation of adoption is not to reify slogans and images. We are quite clearly not the melting pot of American myth and dream. Carl Degler has told us we are far more like a salad bowl, and people who have read and thought much about it now tell us we are beyond the melting pot, and for good reason: the ethnics are unmeltable anyway. I do not trot out grade-school civics recitations when I say that we are a nation of adopters and adoptees. However we have failed generations of immigrants and however far we fall short of our lofty ideals, the simple historical fact is that we are a nation made by choice and not germinated out of the dim and misty regions of the past. Here in America, Edmund Burke's insistence on prescription gave way dramatically to insistence on prediction. In the American experience the important tense has always been the future.

We were not born as other nations were born. We are, as has been said, a creedal nation, not one of blood and time and place. We declared ourselves to be a nation without the usual gestation period. Perhaps no American historian has tried to make us more aware of this than Henry Steele Commager, who has pointed out that the American experience nicely reversed the usual order in appearance of nation and history. Earlier, a history gave birth to a nation; here, the new nation gave birth to a history. So it is with adoption; one does not "inherit" a past, one "appropriates" a past. As H. Richard Niebuhr wrote, "Where common memory is lacking…there can be no real community, and where community is to be formed common memory must be created."

That we are not without ambiguity and even dilemma does not surprise us. More than half a century ago Gunnar Myrdal found the conflict between the American creed and the reality of American racism to be our central dilemma, and others, including C. Eric Lincoln, have continued to hold up that dilemma as a persistent reality in American life. Our national motto is a glorious ideal: *E Pluribus Unum*, from the many, one. We as a nation would resolve one of philosophy's oldest puzzles: the relation of the one to the many. We have not, and it requires little insight to recognize that much of the time the *unum* seems overrun by the *pluribus*. It would be absurd to argue that the United States has effectively and justly incorporated all its constituencies, or that we have yet risen up, as Martin Luther King, Jr., called us to do, to live out our creed. But the indisputable fact remains that as a nation of immigrants we are an adopted and an adopting people. Tragically, the only unadopted Americans were the original settlers mistakenly called Indians by Europeans, and treated as though they were not even human, much less entitled to the land on which they lived. America as "chosen" may or may not have anything to do with divine providence. It has everything to do with how we became and continue as a nation.

Tocqueville saw more than a century and a half ago that part of the social and political genius of American life is its voluntaryism. Americans seem given to voluntary endeavor and are inclined to join groups, and these traits run counter to the ideas of fixed place and heritable station in life. Americans celebrate life as possibility and not fate; we are mobile geographically and socially. We are in demand by groups and organizations, especially churches, who compete for our allegiance. We are expected to "better" ourselves. Granted that the rhetoric of the American Dream celebrates myth as well as reality, as we should expect, it remains that both our official creed and the actual experience of millions embrace a very good analogy to adoption: choice and opportunity. The historic meaning of America derives from a succession of generations who have adopted this land as theirs, and in turn have been, more or less, adopted in return, a meaning Irving Howe has called "the fraternity of all human beings on earth." This historic meaning lives on. During the 1976 bicentennial celebration, I spoke with an English girl in Oxford who held dual citizenship because she had been born in Chicago. She would soon have to decide which permanent citizenship to adopt. I remarked that she would likely cast her lot with England rather than with the United States, would she not? No, Heather replied, she was not at all committed to that course; in fact, she had been thinking seriously about becoming an American citizen by choice, "because of the idea of America."

Give or take a few generations, we have all come from somewhere else. The historic meaning of America is that her sons and daughters were born in other places of other traditions, and that they picked out a new home here. This historical reality helps us to grasp the meaning of adoption. However imperfectly our national life embodies American ideals and dreams, the Statue of Liberty remains a powerful symbol of those ideals and dreams and might be regarded as Our Lady of Adoption, as Ellis Island once served as a national adoption agency.

III

"Through Christ," wrote H. Richard Niebuhr, "we become immigrants into the empire of God which extends over all the world and learn to remember the history of that empire, that is of men in all times and places, as our history." Out of its deficiency and despite its corruption, and out of its Old Testament heritage of "a chosen people," the Christian Church bears witness to the God who created life and who, in the supreme Christian paradox, sent his own Son, Jesus whom Christians call Christ, to redeem and fulfill that life. The church is inclusive, not exclusive; it is cosmopolitan, not parochial; it is universal, not tribal or clannish or racial. All this the church is in its essence and purpose, and in so being illuminates much about the meaning of adoption.

The Christian Church as often as not falls prey to the very parochialism it claims to transcend, and in American life it has borne no greater idolatrous burden than race. Clan and tribe are no strangers to the church, any more than they are strangers to other institutions and organizations. Neither is nation. One cannot proceed very far toward an understanding of religion without recognizing that whatever else it is, religion is a social product and that it bears an unmistakable social stamp. In the United States, with its cultural and religious pluralism, we expect to find evidence of nation and ethnicity in religion, and we are not disappointed. The Roman Catholic Church in the United States is not simply the Catholic Church; it tends to be Irish Roman catholic. Lutheranism, for example, is never simply the Lutheran Church, but is German or Swedish or Danish Lutheranism, depending on where you look.

Nevertheless, the Christian Church claims the ideal of universal brotherhood, knowing with the New Testament writer that the "God that made the world and all things therein" is the God who has "made of one blood all nations." The blood that joins believers is the blood of Christ, shed for all people. Any other distinction according to blood reduces the God and Father of Jesus Christ to a tribal deity and raises the spectre of Aryanism. Contrary to this, Christianity's spiritual transcendence contains the meaning of "the communion of saints," the body of believers in all times and in all places. As with our nation, there is manifold evidence of anything but universality; evidence abounds of provincial and parochial and racial and ethnic exclusiveness. But that is not the nature of the church anymore than it is the faith of our nation. "Who are my mother and my brothers?" asks Jesus. "Here are my mother and my brother! Whoever does the will of God is my brother, and sister, and mother." For St. Paul there is neither slave nor free, neither male nor female, neither Greek nor Jew. "In Christ there is no east or west," says a hymn often sung in Christian congregations, "in him no south or north." The church as ideal embraces all of humankind without distinction, because that is what its Lord proclaimed. Not race, not nation, not clan, not group takes priority over the fellowship of believers who call Jesus "Lord."

Biblical faith insists that God takes the initiative, reaching out to people in divine love incarnate in Jesus of Nazareth and inviting a human response. As God chose to create humanity, so he chose to re-create fallen humanity that it may be once again made whole. We are chosen of God out of His love for us. The New Testament declares this divine initiative by asserting "that while we were yet sinners, Christ died for us." Here is a theology of adoption which illuminates all of life, and which in Biblical passages appears explicitly in the language of adoption. According to the King James version, Ephesians 1:5 says that God "predestinated us unto the adoption of children by Jesus Christ to himself, according to the good pleasure of his will." J. B. Phillips renders the passage in modern English as, "He planned, in his purpose of love, that we should be adopted as his own children through Jesus Christ." The consequence for believers is that "we love because He first loved us." What makes one a person is to be chosen out of love and to love out of choosing. God is a God of adoption. Despite the enormous gap between what the church preaches and practices, blood is not thicker than the water of baptism.

Nothing has so dramatized this claim to universality as the Christian missionary effort, however imperfect. The meaning of Christian missions and evangelism is that one is adopted into the church. The only requirement is to "give your heart to Jesus." In a narrow sense we may say that we are born into the church because our parents were of it and brought us up in it. But even when some form of infant baptism is practiced, those so baptized are expected, when they are presumed to know what they are about, to confirm that baptism, to "own the covenant," as earlier generations had it: to adopt their adoption. The church is a worldwide family of faith in which everyone is chosen.

    To be married is to act out adoption.

    To be American is to applaud adoption.

    To be Christian is to abide through adoption.

Photographs

Demorest, GA 1937

Demorest, GA 1937

Demorest, GA 1940

Putney, VT 1942

Putney, VT 1943

South Willington, CT
2nd Grade 1945

Winter 1948

Dave and Jerome Daugherty
Summer 1955

Following High School
1955

College Cevenol
France 1956

Dave and Nancy
Spring 1962

Dave, Nancy, Margie and
Mama Carol
Merom, IN 1964

Julius Hansen, Lake Sebago
Maine 1967

Alan and Carol, Norway 1970s

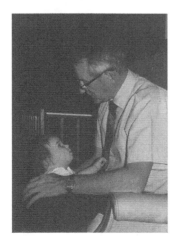

Julius with Rachel 1970   Alan and Carol 1980s

Douglas Hill, Lake Sebago
Maine 1971

Masai Father and Daughter
With Alan, Kenya 1976

Dave, Rey, Brooks and Julius
Rocky Mount, 1973

Dave with George Blackburn and
Peter Hoffman-adopted cousins 1987

Dave 1995

Picking Out The World

"Let's see what Gamal Abdul Nasser has been up to now."

I was sitting in a tent in southern France because my father wanted me to attend an international work camp in Europe the summer after my freshman year at Oberlin. It was his idea, as Oberlin had been, and I at first resisted it. I looked forward to coming back to the familiar surroundings of summer at Merom. He insisted that I go; I didn't know how to refuse. Because I had taken first-year German, it made sense to go to a German-speaking country, and I tried for an opening in Austria. I wound up scheduled for France. I knew no French, but everything would be bilingual during a month at the College Cevenol in Le Chambon sur Lignon. The name and the place meant nothing to me.

The College Cevenol grew out of a school founded in Le Chambon in 1938 by two Protestant pastors. Andre Trocme and Edouard Theis came from the French Huguenot tradition and were committed to non-violence as a way of overcoming evil. Their school, intended to be an international training center for peace and justice in the world, always operated on a shoestring, and following World War II, it hosted international work camps which served two purposes. Young people, and a few older ones, came together from different countries and cultures to do manual labor to help expand school facilities. And they came together to be together. Neither Theis or Trocme was there that summer. Ironically, I later met Trocme in Oberlin while he was on a speaking tour.

People ordinarily do not pay their own way for the privilege of performing manual labor. But the College Cevenol was not ordinary, and people came precisely to work with their hands, using picks and shovels and wheelbarrows, to dig out from a slope the foundation for a new dormitory for the school. We worked hard, but it was fun. Working together bound us into a community of purpose and achievement. Work does that when it is worthwhile.

Most importantly, we embraced each other in a community of mind and spirit, altogether conscious that we were international, interracial, and ecumenical. We did not all agree with everything Trocme and Theis stood for in founding the school. We believed in peace and brotherhood, but not necessarily absolute pacifism. Pacifism challenged us, nevertheless, to rethink whatever alternative to it we proposed, as absolutes always do when not rejected out of hand. And pacifism at Le College Cevenol was incarnate in the hardest-working person among us: a man named Pierre who had been a devoted follower of Andre Trocme, who was on the staff at Le College Cevenol, and who remained committed to Trocme's teaching. Because Pierre had risked his life by following the exhortations of Andre Trocme instead of the dictates of Marshal Petain and the French Vichy regime during World War II, he commanded admiration. His Gallic presence at work and in rigorous discussion meant more than differences of view.

The summer of Le Chambon was unquestionably the great cultural and intellectual divide in my life. I lived and worked and talked with other Americans and with young men and women from Austria, Spain, Holland, France, Lebanon, and various parts of Africa. I was the youngest and surely the most ignorant. Even after a year at Oberlin I felt left out of discussions and debates on foreign policy and political philosophy. That summer in that place among those people I caught the desire to learn. Rudolf, a trilingual Austrian, helped me glimpse what it meant to live after World War II between the Eastern and Western superpowers. John Foster Dulles, the American Secretary of State, was trumpeting the cold-war doctrine that neutralism was immoral. Rudolph taught me otherwise. The Spanish Civil War of the 1930's had been an international ideological cause, and idealistic Americans had no doubt that we should have supported the left to block Franco's rise to power. Elena, who taught Latin and Greek, returned again and again to the war's deepest truth for her: ordinary people suffered terribly to justify someone else's ideology. The young Africans proved daily the silliness of racial and cultural attitudes which concluded that "they" weren't ready for independence and freedom.

My real political education began that morning I sat in a tent between an American graduate of Lehigh University who had been teaching at the American University in Cairo, and a Lebanese Arab who spoke English as well as we did. We had been rained out of our task of digging by hand the foundation of a new building for the school. The American was very pro-Arab in his sympathies: not anti-Semitic, only pro-Arab politically. People in the United States, he said, really didn't know much about the Arabs in the Middle East. They were un-represented in American politics and in the American press. He regularly read the Paris edition of the *New York Herald Tribune* which arrived in Le Chambon a day late, and just now, as we sat there in the tent out of the rain, he opened it to learn that the Egyptian president had nationalized the Suez Canal. He and our Lebanese friend talked of the bold move, back and forth as I sat between them, and I knew I needed to learn more of the world we all lived in. Perhaps as much as anything, that rainy morning persuaded me to major in government when I returned to Oberlin.

It remained for professor Philip Hallie of Wesleyan University to write the story of Le Chambon in a moving book entitled *Lest Innocent Blood Be Shed*, published in 1979. Only then was a connected account of Le Chambon's spiritual vitality and nobility made available. This remarkable vitality was embodied most obviously in Andre Trocme and his wife, and in a less dramatic way in Edouard Theis. The nobility belonged to the entire village. Trocme and Theis led their parishioners, by the faith they shared, in making of Le Chambon a place of refuge for Jews fleeing the persecution of Hitler's Reich. Le Chambon adopted Jews escaping the Holocaust and saved hundreds and thousands of lives.

Back at Oberlin in the fall of 1956, I was vastly more interested in books and ideas. I loved it all: teachers and courses and reading and writing and uncommon friends and imagining I was falling in and out of love. My father worried at first that I would be too quick to marry. Then he worried I would be too slow to marry. I loved Oberlin College and let my father do the worrying. With no clear idea of what to do after graduation and encouraged by a college staff member, I followed my father to Union.

Union Theological Seminary in the early nineteen-sixties was an exciting place for me. On Morningside Heights in New York City, clustered with Columbia University, Barnard College, Julliard before it relocated at Lincoln Center, the Jewish Seminary of America, and Riverside Church, it was part of that area and atmosphere often referred to as the cultural acropolis of America. It was also a symbol of that universal view of the church and the world so precious to my father. Founded by Presbyterians in the 1830's, it had long become interdenominational and just as international. Dozens of ecclesiastical traditions and dozens of countries were represented in its student and faculty community. In truth, the ecumenism of Union was nothing short of militant as it found expression in the person of Henry Pitney Van Dusen, who had succeeded Henry Sloane Coffin as president and who directed the institution's life as energetically as anyone ever coached a team or ran a company. Van Dusen believed, in his own insistent way, that Union was and should be a community. As much despite his pomposity as because of his energy, Union was as true and rich a community as that at Le Chambon, and more sustained because it lasted longer for me. Van Dusen believed just as strongly that its standards should be as demanding as those of any professional academic institution, and he was sure "his faculty" was the best anywhere. He may have been correct in that. We used to laugh and say that if one read a book and failed to understand it, it was simple enough to go down the hall to ask the author what he meant. Union had its stars.

Harry Emerson Fosdick and Reinhold Niebuhr walked side by side down the aisle in the Union chapel at the first ceremony I attended. Here were my father's heroes. Fosdick was in his eighties and retired, but still keen of mind and lively of spirit. It was an honor to meet him. Reinhold Niebuhr was now older than his years. He was virtually retired, though he still lived in his seminary apartment and taught an occasional seminar. I never had the opportunity to claim him as a professor. Even though he had suffered a stroke which marked him with a pronounced limp and somewhat slurred his speech, the power of his presence and the excitement of his ideas were unmistakable. He surmounted his infirmities to make himself available to students for "bull sessions," and he occasionally preached in chapel. Despite his physical decline he was yet a commanding speaker and exciting preacher.

All the stories of his extraordinary capacity to excite interest and compel attention—first-hand accounts from my father and later my teachers at Union and descriptions in books and articles—came alive one day in the seminary refectory. It was a Saturday, late in the lunch hour, and I was eating with one or two friends at a table just beyond the food line at the near end of the dining room. Shortly before the refectory closed, Niebuhr came through, struggling with a tray, and sat down across from me. He scarcely had a chance to eat. People were drifting in and out as he came in, but as soon as he was recognized, everyone came and crowded around him. The empty chairs at the table filled immediately. People stood behind and between them, forming a second rank, and yet behind them those remaining tugged and pulled and strained for a chance to see and hear better. He was purely charismatic, and I could only imagine how he must have been at the peak of his powers. We were too thrilled to let him eat. As Neibuhr held altogether involuntary court, I would not have given up my seat for a month's meals. What he said is lost to memory.

More than anything else, that experience allowed me to grasp what my father had meant when he would tell me about "old Reinie." His features then had been sharp; my father said he had "a nose like an eagle." He brought to the presentation of his ideas, themselves always provocative, a personal energy that charged his listeners intellectually. He did it in conversation, he did it in the classroom, he did it on the lecture circuit, and he did it in the pulpit. The dominant impression one had, even late in his career, was that he was always impatient to get on to the next idea. He simply could not abide wasting time or trivializing opportunities. His impatience undoubtedly helped explain his polemical posture. He was in person kind and gracious and genuinely humble. But intellectually he was ferocious. There is no other word. He attacked sentimentality. He frequently referred to a position or idea as stupid, one of his favorite epithets. Not the person but the position: stupid. Generations of theological students adored him because he was one preacher who could command a hearing from the most prominent intellectuals in the land and in the Western world.

Theology must concern itself with social, political, and economic realities if it were to have any validity for him. He loved to talk politics. He had, after all, influenced American political thought decisively. In the Spring of 1960, before the national party conventions, again surrounded in the refectory, he was discussing the American political scene.

"Nixon is dishonest," he announced, "and Kennedy is an operator."

I saw him early in the following term and reminded him of that pronouncement.

"Well, Dr. Niebuhr," I said, "it looks as if you're stuck and won't be able to vote."

"Oh, no," growled the man who had once threatened to retire to a monastery if Nixon were elected president of the United States, "I'll vote for Kennedy," and paused before continuing, "but with very little enthusiasm."

I had planned to spend the following summer in Colorado, combining a church job with construction work. I went home instead because my father said he needed me. It was embarrassing to withdraw from the Colorado commitment, and even more embarrassing to discover, after his death, a letter from my father explaining to my prospective employer in Colorado that I wouldn't be much good out there anyway. Such a letter was dishonest and uncalled for, but it reminded me of how tense my father had become. His future and that of Merom Institute seemed uncertain to him. He was now in his late fifties and felt a financial strain from buying and renovating the first house he and my mother had ever owned. He felt imposed on by the Board of Trustees, and more than that he felt that his entire work and ministry at Merom Institute were now implicitly called into question by decisions of the board that he did not agree with or believe in. He could not bring himself to let it show, and it ate at him from the inside. So I went home.

His appeal for me to return to Merom was a cry for help. I realized that he felt deserted by his administrative superiors, and I knew he must not feel deserted by me. I knew also that he exaggerated the fault he assigned to those superiors. He was not blameless for increasing tension between him and the board. He could be stubborn and inflexible. Worse, he sometimes retreated to a mood of pious sincerity from which no appeal to reason or evidence could recall him. I knew this, but what mattered was that my father needed me. I might have felt cheated of a promising opportunity in Colorado, but I didn't. Instead I felt only a need to help. Once I was back home I realized that he required my emotional and psychological support, not my help at the Institute. Briefly, the roles of father and son were reversed. He needed me for no job; he needed me close by to confirm the meaning of his life. And so I went home.

My roommate during my second year at Union was a Mississippian named Rinaldo Addison Lansdell Walker, known to everyone as Bud. Bud Walker was a gifted man who would direct the ministry of the North Carolina prison system. Throughout the term I reported to him on the news from home, and told him much of my family history. We were both Southerners by birth, though my adoption early took me north. Now and then in bits and pieces I described the family and home life I had come to take for granted. To be loved unconditionally was how it should be, wasn't it? I would tell him about going home for Christmas vacation during college, and drinking hot tea with my mother, especially after we moved to old Doc Woodworth's place, where my father had the hill top sliced off so we could see the Illinois side of the river from our house. Bud always listened closely and smiled in what seemed genuine appreciation. He said, now and then, that my father sounded a little like St. Francis. It never occurred to me Bud thought I made it all up.

But he did. My father appeared early one morning unexpectedly at our rooms. He had come east to get his mother to take her back to Merom to live with him and my mother, and he wanted to see me at Union. He was in good spirits. I woke Bud, and he staggered out of his room bleary-eyed to meet my father. He told me later that until that moment he thought I had fabricated the whole thing, that I suffered from being rejected—I was, after all, adopted—and compensated by inventing a wildly unrealistic home life. My family, and especially my father, couldn't be real. Just meeting him, seeing him and speaking with him briefly, he said, confirmed all I had told him. Right then he gave my father the name we called him by ever since.

"Daddy Alan really is real," said Bud.

The summer after that second year at Union saw me in a rural parish in southern Illinois about two hours from Merom. My father appeared stronger and more confident. I drove up to see him and my mother about once a month. Nick Johnston had come to work at the Institute for the summer, and was immensely helpful to my father.

I returned to Union for my final year braced to write a required thesis and assuming I would then move on to a parish. Probably because I had grown up there, I assumed that my ministry would be in rural America: what our denomination called "the church in town and country." Before beginning serious work on the thesis and before thinking much about parish possibilities, I met a first-year student from Atlanta named Nancy Brooks and quickly decided I wanted to marry her. That year at Union would have been a good one in any event. My roommate, Walt Herbert, as much as anyone yet sharpened my mind, and the burden of my thesis on Washington Gladden became a joy. It would have been a good year. When Nancy agreed to marry me, she made it glorious.

Washington Gladden was the "father of the social gospel" in America. Encouraged by John Bennett, I now "worked on" Gladden and submitted the thesis to him and Roger Shinn. It was special to me that John Coleman Bennett, so long an inspiration to my father, had now become my own mentor as well. He had "corrected," as my father put it, his thesis more than thirty years earlier as a young tutor, and now he would read mine. It was my greatest academic satisfaction at Union.

"You've really made him live," John Bennett told me when we met in the Hall.

A few days later I was called to the phone just outside my room. It was John Bennett.

"Dr. Shinn and I have just read your thesis and we want to put it in the library."

I felt anointed. I assumed that when I gave my thesis over to my professors it represented the last serious work of its kind I would do. I anticipated no further formal study, and I never then dreamed of becoming a professor. I would write sermons and reports and letters and perhaps an article now and then. The Union Seminary thesis was a proper conclusion to my academic life. Now it was on to professional life as a parish minister. John Bennett's call and announcement of his and Roger Shinn's estimation of my work was the perfect consummation of my academic life at Union. I thanked him and rushed to tell Walt. His response lifted me still higher.

"I'm not surprised," he said. "I know you are capable of that quality of work."

Nancy hugged me, and it remained only to share the thesis and the good news with my father. My mother would be pleased, but he would find it special. He would, I knew, see immediately its source in what he had said to me that day on the campus of Merom Institute outside Gladden Cabin. And he would be especially pleased that I had dedicated it to him: "For A. T. J. who first told me about Washington Gladden." I had reported on its progress and completion but I had intentionally kept from him my dedication. I wanted to surprise him when I could hand him the finished and approved manuscript. He and my mother were coming east to New York for my graduation and a visit with the relatives in Watchung. I planned to show it to him out there at Ernie and Lucy's house.

My father enjoyed our time at Union. He had lunch together with Wilhelm Pauck, whom he had known for years and who had taught me. He saw his old friend Daniel Day Williams, whom he knew from Williams's time on the faculty at the Chicago Theological Seminary. He met James Muilenburg, whose commentary on Second Isaiah in the Interpreter's Bible so impressed him. I introduced him to Robert McAfee Brown, who would speak at commencement. And of course he renewed his friendship with John Bennett. Union was good for him, but he was tired and worried.

We left New York after the graduation exercise and went out to Watchung to spend the night before heading home to Merom the next day. Everybody knew that my parents regularly went early to bed, but even they stayed up later than usual. Everyone had a good time. Everyone except my father. He was preoccupied. Still, I thought this was the time. I presented him with a copy of the thesis.

"John Bennett and Roger Shinn liked it enough to have it placed in the Union library," I said as I handed it to him. I wanted to see his response when he opened it to the dedication.

He took it without registering any emotion. I stood next to him, relatives moving about and talking, and watched him just look at the black springboard cover that bound the pages, and then slowly and absently open it. I knew he was tired and worried, but was just as certain that the dedication would enliven him. He started to turn the page.

"Look," I said, "look at the dedication page."

He fumbled for it and I found it for him. He looked at it. There it was, alone on the page: "For A. T. J. who first told me about Washington Gladden." His page, my gift. He looked at it as I looked at him. Nothing, there was nothing. He didn't show anything and he didn't say anything. He just stood there. Then he closed the cover and handed it back to me. It was too late, I thought, for him to concentrate, too late for him to do anything but go to bed.

"Well," I said, "I hope you'll enjoy reading it." I gave it back to him. "This is your copy, you can keep it. I made it for you."

"I'm very tired," he said.

"I know. Read it when you want to."

He never did. He never read the thesis I wrote for John Bennett and dedicated to him. Years later in Theodore Rosengarten's superb *All God's Dangers*, I read what Nate Shaw said of his father, that he "never did in his lifetime notice my crop." My father once wrote me in college that he would die for me, and I believed him, but he never read my thesis.

He was physically and emotionally exhausted from the strain he now felt in his job. Following our marriage in Atlanta, which he helped to perform, he and my mother left Merom Institute and their home to our keeping and went abroad for a vacation, the first real one they had ever had. The days in Atlanta for the wedding pleased him; he was happy for us and certain I had picked out a splendid mate. But he needed help at home and rest.

They returned at the end of the summer, and he, considerably refreshed, performed part of my ordination ceremony. He who had so often seemed ambivalent about things I had done and so uncertain of commending me, was unrestrained when he told me how well I had read a paper and fielded questions. He said then and often told me later that it was one time I was at my best. He made no personal comparison with himself or abstract comparison with an ideal. He praised me.

He said later, and Nancy and I and my mother could only agree, that his very life may have hung in the balance until he went away for that summer. He was tired in his bones. He was worn out because he no longer felt properly supported by the people charged with overseeing the work of Merom Institute. For them it was a new day and no longer his day. He who had become, in Edward Ouellette's phrase, the very "spirit of Merom," now felt pressured to leave. It didn't make it easier for him that he was nearly sixty.

So he was tired and didn't read my thesis that summer. He never read it. I remarked on this years later to my mother, when they had moved to Maine and a wonderful new season in their shared life. I told her I was disappointed that he had never got around to it. She said he was very tired and near a breakdown at the time of my graduation. I said I knew that, but I was sorry he had not read it since. Later, again in Maine, he spoke with me about it one evening as we sat together in his study.

"There's something I want to bring up," he said, leaning back in his swivel chair as he always had when we were in his study and he had something to say to me. "I heard a while back that you were ticked off with me for not reading your thesis."

He meant, of course, that my mother had spoken to him. That I had been "ticked off"' was his own inference and elaboration. He clasped his hands behind his head in that way I had seen so often, and he affected the grave manner which was too close to comic to call.

"You don't know how tired I was at that time," he continued. "I was close to collapse. Things were not going well at the Institute. I was not getting along with some of the people in charge and some of their decisions hurt me."

I knew that was true. It hurts when your father is hurt, and he had been. Had he forgotten that Nancy and I spent the summer there precisely so he could get away from it all? I knew, but I no longer knew whether he knew.

"I just didn't have the strength to do it. I just couldn't read it. There was too much else on me."

I may never know whether I did the right thing. I said simply that I knew he had been tired and under considerable pressure. That is all I said and he dropped it. I hadn't the heart to point out that it had been years ago, that in the decade since then, and especially because he was so disciplined a reader, he could have found time for it. Or that he might have taken it on one of the trips he and my mother since then had frequently enjoyed. I hadn't the heart and said nothing and neither of us ever brought it up again. After his death my mother explained to Nancy that I did not understand "how sick dad had been," and that is why he never read the thesis. "David just doesn't realize how bad it was." No more than I had with my father did Nancy have the heart to tell my mother that we had spent the summer in Merom precisely because we did know he was sick and needed desperately to get away. And she too simply passed over the most obvious thing of all: that two decades had elapsed since that summer.

A further irony was lost on my mother. Always proud of my father, she took special pleasure in his regular reading habits and talked often of the many books he read, and how he was always ordering them from lending libraries as well as buying them. She was proud of his books and his insistence that he must read to stay alive and alert mentally and spiritually. How could he preach without reading? She had been conditioned to leave him undisturbed from the time he rose from his afternoon nap until four o'clock, when they regularly went for a swim. He must read. All this she embraced willingly. She bragged on it. It never occurred to her that my father chose not to pick up and read my thesis.

After he died, when I went through his papers I found a copy of a letter to his mother in which he wrote, "Dave's thesis rated an A." I discovered also the copy of the thesis I had given him. There was a marker about a third of the way through its ninety-five pages. I don't know whether it was there coincidentally or whether he actually had begun to read it. He told me only that he couldn't read it when I gave it to him. From that moment until he died more than twenty years later, he had never taken two hours—if indeed it would have required that much—to read what I wrote for John Bennett and dedicated to him.

I mentioned it to a friend after his death, who said he must have been afraid to read it. That had not occurred to me. She said he must have feared the implicit comparison with his own time and work at Union, and what I took as a personal satisfaction and compliment to him, he may have feared as an achievement he never reached. I didn't know then and I don't know now.

In September of 1962 Nancy and I went to Granville, Illinois, about one hundred miles southwest of Chicago and population one thousand, to a United Church of Christ pastorate. Our first child, Marjorie, was born in 1964, and a year later we left Granville for Evanston, Illinois, where I had been invited to join a Methodist church staff, and we could do graduate work. We enrolled in Northwestern University for master's degree programs, Nancy in English and I in Religion, and I then decided to continue on for a doctorate in American history. I left the church staff with mixed feelings only a year and a half after joining it. We had loved the work, primarily with young people, but there were growing tensions on the job.

A month before leaving the church, I went to a dentist with what felt like an impacted wisdom tooth. He diagnosed the difficulty as TMJ and made an appointment for me to see a psychologist on the University of Illinois Circle Campus in Chicago, explaining that "it's partly hereditary and partly individual." Mystified, I made my way to the doctor's office. He welcomed me genially and presented me with a set of psychological tests. I asked if we understood each other, that I had a bad jaw. He smiled as professionals do who know their business. Take the tests, he said pleasantly but firmly, and then we'll talk.

"You see," said the doctor when I had finished and returned the tests to him, "you have a problem we call TMJ, short for tempero mandibular joint dysfunction. In part, your difficulty lies in a defective jaw structure; there's nothing you could do to prevent that. You were born with it. It is congenital."

Ah, I realized, that's the heredity part. The doctor hurried on to say that the important thing, which the tests were designed to help locate, was why this hereditary deficiency had lately become a problem.

"You see," he said, "we have learned that what activates TMJ, what in fact causes the problem, is not something physiological, but something psychological."

"You mean," I blurted out, "it's sort of like an ulcer?"

He was blank for a moment, and then replied that yes, it is rather of the order of an ulcer. But one step at a time. Because the psychological something affected an already present physiological condition which was congenital, it might be helpful to recall whether anyone else in my family, especially either of my parents, had suffered from the condition.

"Oh," I said brightly, "that doesn't work in my case, Doctor. I'm adopted."

"You're <u>adopted</u>," he said, more than asked. He almost cooed, "Tell me about it."

"Well, it's simple enough," I said. "When I was ten days old I was adopted by my mother and father."

"Don't you mean that you were adopted <u>from</u> your mother and…father?" The pause told me he may have regretted adding "father."

Innocence dies hard in the presence of a psychologist.

"Oh, no," I said, more brightly than ever, "my mother and father adopted me, my mom and dad." I rushed on. "I don't have any brothers or sisters, so the three of us are our family."

He became grave.

"Tell me," he said, "something about your…family."

"I can never remember not being loved."

The professional before me seemed unprepared for that. It didn't fit his grid. Later, I realized it was Bud Walker all over again. Here is this boy fabricating a fantasy to compensate for an unhappy childhood.

"David," he said, "we know that TMJ is a psychological problem. When it occurs, something is wrong. Now you say you are an adopted child."

"Yes," I cut in, "as I told you my mother and father adopted me when I was ten days old." I smiled directly at him.

"But we must discover what is troubling you, what has caused your jaw to tighten and cause you pain."

Now I knew. Something intangible was affecting me tangibly. It was simple. I had failed to handle the ambivalence and strain of my job, even though I had resigned months ago and was within a few weeks of leaving it.

"David," he said, "I think I know I what your difficulty is. I think you're look-ing for your father."

"You think what?" I was incredulous.

"I think you're looking for your father. It's natural enough, and we often find it in adopted children. It's not unusual at all for an adult, such as yourself, to want to find his real father."

Everything converged for me now—my jaw, the doctor's assumptions, and most importantly, the shape of my life.

"That's silly," I said, "plain silly. I'm not looking for my father. I'm quitting a job."

"David, often people do not understand what motivates them, what 'makes them tick.' And just as often they have difficulty accepting reality. People ration-alize, they say one thing to conceal another."

"Doctor," I broke in, "can you give me something for my jaw? Can anybody give me something for my jaw?"

"Yes," he said, "we will fit you with a mouthpieces that will ease the symptoms of your distress. But the important thing is to locate the cause of it."

I told him I had located it. And then I applied to myself a word I had always thought belonged to others.

"I am feeling and showing the effects of stress."

He was so certain. It was classic.

"The stress you are experiencing as TMJ has its source, I'm quite confident, in the search for your father."

"Doctor, you really have been helpful. If you'll just give me the mouthpiece I'll get back home and explain it all to my wife. She was a psychology major in col-lege. She'll get it right away, and I think she'll find it interesting."

"David, you're a complex person. If you can accept the fact that because you are adopted, you wonder about your origins, you have a natural curiosity about where you came from, you want to discover your father—if you can do this, whether you ever find him or not—I think you can manage the TMJ problem."

"Doctor," I said, "I don't want to offend you, but that's a lot of crap. Good God, I know my father and always have. Now if you'll just get me that mouth-piece and tell me what to do and what not to do, I'll be very grateful."

"David, I don't want to offend you either, but I have a professional obligation to give you the benefit of my deepest insight and best advice. I must say I think you will be disappointed and will discover that your difficulty will continue."

"I'll tell you what," I said, beginning to sympathize with him, "I'll tell you what I'll do. You give me the mouthpiece and any instructions I need, and if it doesn't work I'll get back in touch with you. I promise."

"We'll have to measure your mouth," he said with a sigh, and sent me down the hall to a technician. Fitted out with a toothless upper plate, I returned to his office. It was all a bit mysterious, but I was to wear it except when eating and sleeping. I should avoid chewy things for awhile, such as challenging cuts of meat, and by all means was I to stop chewing gum. That could tie my jaw in a knot. Wear the appliance for two or three months, he said. That should be enough to tell the story. He wasn't convinced, but he accepted a momentary standoff and wished me well. I thanked him, and his young Telemachus went home.

That was in June, 1966. I left the job in July, wore the mouthpiece faithfully, and ate gentle food. I stopped chewing gum cold turkey. It worked. Once, a couple of months later, my jaw locked on a bit of steak, and in October I tried a piece of gum. The doctor had been right; it was excruciating. I haven't chewed since. I never understood how the mouthpiece worked, but I was delivered from the jaws of TMJ. So much for the search for the father.

Just after we moved to Evanston, my father and mother moved to Maine. Merom Institute was no longer his and he had left as its Director at the beginning of 1964. He was sixty years old and uncertain of his future, but he knew the Institute was now the past. He would take his chances in rural churches, near enough for him to serve while he and my mother lived in their home on the Merom bluff. The very next year "from out of the blue," as he unoriginally said it, came an opportunity to take over a church conference center in Maine. It was perfect for him and my mother after their years in Merom, and it opened a rich and creative chapter in their lives that continued until my father died. We left

Granville for Evanston, and they left the banks of the Wabash for the shores of Lake Sebago.

My father was back in his glory. Besides managing Rockcraft Lodge, he made himself available for preaching, and until the last summer of his life he would fill pulpits. He assumed a succession of pastorates and also served churches as an interim minister. At Rockcraft Lodge he and my mother did what they were best at by welcoming people to a spiritual home away from home. They lived simply in what had been the caretaker's cottage on the estate that became a church center.

He was permitted to remain at Rockcraft for a year beyond the mandatory retirement age for an official of the Maine Conference United Church of Christ. Meanwhile, he and my mother had bought a summer home across the lake just outside of North Windham, which they winterized and moved into in 1969 to "retire." In fact, that meant only relinquishing the duties at Rockcraft. My father had always said, or boasted, that he would likely "die in the harness." He had no intention of giving up his work as preacher and pastor.

We went to see them each summer, usually by way of Watchung. My Hughes grandparents and Uncle Casper had died; Ernie and Lucy still lived in their house and Helen in hers up on Hughes Lane. George had married Pat Peacock, whom he met at Oberlin, in 1950. Kim was born in 1954, and the month I went off to Oberlin, Greg was born in an iron lung because Pat had contracted polio. Miraculously both mother and son lived, but Pat remained paralyzed until she died thirty-two years later, dividing her time between a rocker bed and a mechanized wheelchair equipped with an apparatus to stimulate her breathing. Life rarely turns out as we plan, but George and Pat lived a magnificent testimony to hope in the house George had built just below his mother's on the hill.

From their new home my parents returned to the parish ministry together. Increasingly my father had to limit his work, and he became more and more insistent on being protected from intrusion. But he kept at it. He loved the life of a minister, and my mother remained his loyal helper. They made friends in the little community where they now lived, and in a succession of churches. Maine was a second wind and a new life for him. So close to collapse, and perhaps nearer than we knew to becoming embittered back in Merom in the early sixties, he now found a new usefulness and confirmation as a spiritual leader and interpreter of life's meaning.

I, too, was fortunate. Edmund Perry guided me through the master's program and aimed me toward the doctorate. In the Northwestern history department I found myself among a constellation of stars: Christopher Lasch, George Frederickson, and Robert Wiebe. Lasch made history possible for me, and Frederickson and Wiebe guided me more deeply into its American meaning. Meanwhile our two other children, Brooks and Rachel, were born, and in 1971 I accepted an offer to teach American history at North Carolina Wesleyan College in Rocky Mount, North Carolina.

During our last year in Evanston I was an assistant to the chaplain at Northwestern University, and assumed along with other responsibilities occasional preaching duties. My mother and father came to visit one weekend when I was to preach. On Saturday I took him over to the campus to see the chapel: a modern structure which yet faintly evoked the Gothic, dominated by a stained glass mural looming up at the back of the chancel. I let us into the narthex with the key that went with my job, and then led him through the double doors that opened onto the center aisle of the sanctuary. He just stood there and looked around, and when he spoke, his tone was filled with wonder.

"I've never preached in a place like this."

We were racing again.

He and my mother and Nancy and some friends came to the service the next day, and afterward back in our home we talked about it. My father said nothing and seemed withdrawn, especially if anyone mentioned the sermon. Someone complimented me on it and I laughed and said that dad seemed not to agree. He protested quite unconvincingly.

Modest legacies enabled my mother and father to travel almost annually after they moved to Maine. He was on the lookout for theological seminars in Europe advertising special rates, and for opportunities to sail inexpensively by freighter. They loved it. They spent summers on the Continent and in Britain, traveling either by Eurail pass or in a rented car. Guided tours were not for them. He loved getting onto the back roads in Germany and breaking out his German on farmers and villagers. Always, he was sure there was a story waiting to be discovered. Always, he and my mother acted out their conviction that the human family is one, near and far, and it must be embraced. They took boat trips in the Caribbean, once on a Russian ship, and went to Russia. Even their unstinting optimism could not brighten the gray mood they sensed in the Soviet Union.

They wouldn't stop. In 1976 they journeyed to Nairobi, Kenya, for the World Council of Churches meeting. My father felt increasingly that white Westerners needed to know more of the Third World, and when they returned he prodded us to get out there and see where the future was: not in the old capitals of Europe, but in Africa and Asia. Two pictures from that trip capture perfectly his ecumenical spirit. A slide has him flanked by John Brademas, then an Indiana congressman and later the president of New York University, and Margaret Meade. A photograph shows him in rural Kenya wearing a funny hat to protect his head from the sun and standing between two natives: a "Masai father and daughter who hitchhiked with us for forty miles," as he labeled the back of the photo. The African father looks toward the camera impassively, while his daughter reveals the beginnings of a smile. My father is grinning between them, beneath his funny hat, as they stand at the roadside before re-boarding their bus. He is showing whoever looks at the photograph that this is more than a holiday: it is a glimpse of the future. He came from that meeting of the World Council of Churches most of all impressed by something said by a fellow American, James Cone, the Black liberation theologian. "You've read the books," he told me Cone had declared to the assembly, "but you haven't read me." In the photograph between the two Masai, my father is "reading" Black Africa, and saying to us all that we had better read her too.

The following year he and my mother went around the world on a "Semester at Sea" sponsored by the University of Colorado. They sailed on the *S. S. Universe*, once more acting out their conviction that one was never through picking out experiences necessary to keep growing in mind and spirit. They stopped in Asian ports, and in Hong Kong informally acquired a "Chinese granddaughter" named Janice Chou to whom my mother wrote as long as she was able.

They planned a trip to Norway and Britain for the summer of 1978, but Nancy and I were sure a heart attack my father had in February would keep them home. I talked by phone with him while he was still in the hospital in Portland, Maine, and tried to suggest that it might be time to close out the international traveling that had become such a staple of their lives. He would not hear of it. He had a few months to recover and was confident he would be up to the trip. It was not the time for indirection. I had to confront him.

"Dad," I said, trying to picture him lying abed in the hospital, "you have to realize that you'll be running a serious risk if you go. You aren't young any more and you've had a heart attack." I was thinking of my mother as well as of him. "You can't afford to ignore it."

He came right back in a firm voice, and his response at once relieved and inspired me.

"What's the use of having your life if you don't use it for something."

"You're right."

They took the trip, and he became so ill my mother thought he would die. That didn't stop him. They cruised the Caribbean and saw Haiti's seemingly hopeless poverty. Here again was the Third World he was sure contained the future. He continued to talk of travel and discovery still to come, but even he now had to make concessions to time and health. Following the heart attack he and my mother were obliged to go south for the winters. Annually they stopped off to visit us in Rocky Mount on their way down to Florida in the fall and on their way back north in the spring.

The last journey my father undertook was one of mind and spirit. "There is no frigate like a book," wrote Emily Dickinson, and she could have had him in mind. Slowed by age and increasingly forced to protect his weak heart, he read extensively in Roman Catholic theology: Karl Rahner, the great German scholar whose published work was so massive it defied explanation; Edward Schillebeeckx, the immensely creative Dutch thinker; and most of all Hans Kung, the Swiss Catholic who so persuasively interpreted the theology of his country-man Karl Barth, one of Protestantism's modern giants, and who positioned himself in critical tension with the Vatican. If my father had one final mentor it was Hans Kung. He pronounced *On Being a Christian* a great book.

He and my mother had picked me out to be their child. As I grew up, adoption meant more than the fact of our family. Adoption promised possibilities whose only limit was a defective imagination or a faulty nerve. Even as it informed my self-understanding and helped shape my view of the world, adoption continued to extend itself in their experience until it embraced the world itself.

Julius

"The barber has read Reinhold Niebuhr," I yelled as I rushed into our new home in Granville, Illinois.

"What?" called my wife from a room away.

"The barber has read Reinhold Niebuhr."

I grinned as I found her and she looked suspicious.

"What are you talking about?"

"It's true," I said, "the barber has read Niebuhr. I just met him and he took me to his house and he's read Niebuhr."

It was, as someone in the eighteenth century might have said, rather too wonderful. This was a few days after we arrived in Granville and I had just met Julius Hansen. I walked into his barber shop on Main Street to learn that he knew who I was before I could introduce myself. Granville was a small town.

"Hi, Dave. How are you? Sit down for a minute. I'll take a break and we'll go up the street for a coke."

Just like that. He introduced me to his partner and we all talked about fishing, which they both cared for and I didn't, and baseball, which we all loved, while he finished with the customer he was working on. Julius was about five feet eight, slender, and appeared to be about sixty years old. He had a good face: clean profile, firm features, strong and steady eyes. Right away I could see that he cared not only for the way he made his customers look, but for how he looked himself. He was not careless of appearances and impressions. Casual, but not careless. He brushed himself off, told his partner we would be back soon, and we went out the door.

He led me up to the corner and into the drugstore where we sat down on stools at the counter, and he ordered coffee and I a coke. He paid. He lit a cigarette and we sipped at the drinks. He was already anxious to leave and insisted that I let him show me where he lived. We drove in his Mustang to a tiny bungalow two blocks away. It is remarkable how easily and quickly we had come to his home. Only a few minutes before, I had first seen him in his barber shop. I followed him into the house, and there on a small table to the left of the door was Reinhold Niebuhr's *The Nature and Destiny of Man*.

"Julius," I exclaimed, "you have read Niebuhr!" It was incredible to me. "Have you actually read this book?"

"Yes, I've read Reinie." He used the nickname friends and admirers of Niebuhr employed. "I think he's quite a guy."

He knew Niebuhr had taught at Union Seminary for many years, and that I had just graduated from Union, but he could not have known whether I had ever met him or taken a course with him or read his books. And he could not have known how profoundly Niebuhr had influenced me, and the esteem in which I held him. C. S. Lewis says in *The Four Loves* that "friendship is about something." Julius and I had just become friends.

He was charged up to show me his library, and I saw books which today I affectionately number among my own. He had read Vernon Parrington's massive *Main Currents in American Thought*, a much-used college text in the 1930's and 1940's, which presented the American experience as a struggle between the forces of light and those of darkness, and in which Thomas Jefferson stood forth as the grand champion of enlightened thought and democratic spirit and hope. He had Henry George's *Progress and Poverty*, William Allen White's *Autobiography*, and Alpheus Mason's life of Louis Brandeis. There were books by T. V. Smith, that doughty champion of democracy and the people, and many more. Julius was a reader and wanted someone to talk to about books and ideas, and the new minister at his church was a good prospect. He had obviously brought me to his house for me to see his books, and he probably placed Niebuhr in conspicuous view deliberately. I was hooked. Niebuhr in the house of the barber.

"Julius, where did you go to college?"

"I didn't."

It was even more marvelous.

He was born in Denmark, on the island of Bornholm, and came to the United States when he was eighteen years old. He did not know English when he arrived, and a man in Ottawa, Illinois, advised him to read the *Chicago Tribune* to help him learn the language. The people who wrote it knew their craft, said his advisor. Julius came to detest the point of view represented by the *Trib*, but his friend had been right, and it helped Julius learn English as he learned the barber's trade. Here he was in Granville, where he had been cutting hair and reading books since his early twenties. He was sixty-one years old. How better to sum him up to my wife than to announce that the barber had read Reinhoid Niebuhr?

Julius was not much of a church-goer. He had, in effect, married into the then Congregational Church, now the United Church of Christ, and while his wife was alive, he attended church with her. But it was on her account and not out of any deep conviction or desire. He had been "turned off" to the organized church when he was a boy in Denmark. His Lutheran pastor had criticized him severely in his confirmation class for raising questions about the truth and verifiability of doctrines propounded in the class. Julius often told us that this experience, when he was twelve, had been one of defining significance in his life. If the church was where questions were not allowed, then he would have to find a spiritual home elsewhere.

He was a born visionary, and the American tradition he appropriated, much of it from the pages of Parrington, fed his seeker's soul. Robert Ingersoll, the nineteenth-century American iconoclast, was one of his heroes, and he rather imagined himself in the role of the small-town man of mind constantly beset by bigotry and provincialism, but urged on by the ghosts of Jefferson and Ingersoll. Julius was not a crusader and he was not very embattled; he was short on intellectual companionship. He cared for common decency, desired justice, and scorned ecclesiastical distinctions. When the local priest twitted him for attending the Congregational Church, which he characterized as "next to nothing," Julius retorted that the only reason he was there was the absence of a Unitarian congregation, to which the priest replied "nothing at all." He was committed to what he took to be the message of the Bible and the professed witness of the church: the fatherhood of God and the brotherhood of man. But he never really recovered, as others have not, from the abject authoritarianism he felt so heavily as a boy. He doubted that a state church, as the Lutheran Church was in Denmark, could embody spiritual vitality and intellectual curiosity. And he was suspicious, again following Jefferson and Ingersoll, of any very substantial claim to truth levied by an ecclesiastical organization.

"Can we know the absolute truth?" he would say, the question really a pronouncement that we couldn't. When he gave me Clinton Rossiter's *Seedtime of the Republic* for Christmas, he inscribed it: "to Dave the searcher. May he never think that he knows the ultimate answers." So, effectively, he left the church. But not quite. His wife brought him back, literally, and we drew him to it again. He realized that our social and intellectual motivation lay in our pilgrimage of faith, and he respected this, just as we respected his skepticism. He need not embrace our claims of faith, but if he were to be honest he would have to recognize their importance for us. We got on splendidly.

He married late, when he was past forty, following a courtship of seventeen years. There were two reasons for this unorthodox timing. The lady he wooed was a schoolteacher who loved her teaching as well as him, and the law in Illinois at the time forbade her to continue in her job if she married. The other reason was that he wanted to reduce the likelihood of children. He would not have any, absolutely. His European heritage bore upon him here. He said it plainly. He refused to contribute cannon fodder—his term—to the world's wars. He had seen too much war and too much tragic loss of life, and wanted no part of it. He became wonderfully fond of our children, and seemed to know that for us they were signs of hope and not futility. But he would have none of his own. So he waited to marry, and then wed a woman five years older than he. His wife had died four years before we met. Although he had two brothers in Illinois, one nearby and the other about fifty miles away, he was not close to either, and the loss of his wife left him grief-stricken.

Julius would regularly come over to the parsonage on Saturday evenings after he had closed up the barber shop and gone home to clean up. Often he stopped at the tavern on Main Street to pick up three take-out dinners. The choices were chicken or shrimp, and we leaned toward chicken. He would call on Thursday or

Friday, if one of us had not seen him down at his shop or on the street, to be sure we planned to be home, and he would offer to pick up some "tavern chicken." He was sure that if one of us were seen entering or leaving the tavern we'd be in trouble with some of our parishioners. We laughed and let him bring the food. Sometimes Nancy would fix supper. And now and then we would go over to the 101 Club in LaSalle, only fifteen minutes away, for a good meal at a low price. He would ask the waitress for a steak bone to take home to our new Labrador retriever "Tiamat," named for the dragon of chaos in the Babylonian creation story. Julius and Tiamat became good friends. There we were on a Saturday night, eating and usually watching "The Defenders," and finally folding the bulletins, which Nancy had typed and mimeographed, for the Sunday service. Almost always the next morning he would appear in church.

His spirit grew livelier and he began to write poetry, usually inspired by conscience or romantic imagination, and sometimes with pronounced religious images and implications. He was everyone's friend in Granville, but he took a special delight in his younger companions, most of them—besides us—local high-school teachers just out of college. He was in love with a young English teacher, but feared ridicule from the town and rejection by her if he admitted it. So he kept it to himself except for a poem we knew she inspired.

In His Loneliness
He Created The universe.
In A Moment Of Weakness Man.
At His Very Best He created woman.
Yet It Took From Eve Until You
For God To Be pleased.

He felt freer to be open and share ideas with younger people. It was as if, having come from Europe to a young country, he would keep himself young in mind and spirit by becoming friends with young men and women. One of his fondest and firmest convictions was that the truth, even though we couldn't know it absolutely, could and would win out in the "marketplace of ideas." We—Nancy and I and the young teachers—were part of his marketplace in Granville.

He followed Jefferson in this conviction, doubtless influenced by Parrington, the expositor of the Jeffersonian persuasion par excellence. His Jeffersonian bias sometimes got out of hand, and at least once ran riot. When Jones and Laughlin announced the construction of a large steel plant six miles away on the Illinois River, *The New York Times* ran a story on it for which Julius was interviewed. He feared the new plant as Jefferson had feared the workshops of Europe, should they be transplanted to the United States.

"We are now living here the good life," Julius was quoted as saying, "the simple agrarian life."

Nancy and I howled.

"Listen, Jules," I said, "you may be living the good life in Granville, but you aren't living the simple agrarian life. The simple agrarian life is getting up on a cold morning, lighting a candle, building a fire to cook and heat water you've pumped from a well, and going outside to feed the stock. What do you do? You get up to a mechanical alarm clock, switch on an electric light, draw hot water from a faucet to wash your face, and shave with an electric razor. Then you get dressed, in a house automatically heated to a temperature you desire, walk out to your garage, get in your Mustang, and drive downtown to the cafe for breakfast. Whatever that is, Jules, it is not the simple agrarian life."

He came back at me by insisting that a large new plant could seriously alter the life of the community. That much was true, and we knew he cared about it. We also knew it pleased him to have been selected by the *Times* for an interview, a pleasure increased by *Business Week*, which also covered the story, when it ran his picture.

Julius had little confidence in politicians, though he was one himself and continued to hope that the political system would produce more justice and less inequality. He stuck with the dream. He had long been active in county and municipal politics, respected and trusted by everyone. He loved to laugh and tell us of the time he walked past two elderly women chatting on a front porch and overheard one of them tell the other, "you can tell by looking that Julius is good." I am sure he always voted for Democratic presidential candidates, but in Putnam County, Illinois, one must be a declared Republican to win. He often denounced to us, privately, Senator Everett Dirksen, whom many regarded as Illinois' finest contribution to Washington since Abraham Lincoln. Julius couldn't stand Dirksen's vocal dramatics, which he was sure were phony, and more than that, he was convinced that Dirksen was committed to the status quo and unwilling to risk anything for the poor and the denied. Julius had once asked him, when Dirksen was campaigning for office, why it would not be proper to draft materiel, since it was permissible and even patriotic to draft human beings. He never forgave Dirksen his one-word response: "communism."

So here was Julius L. Hansen, the L. for Ludwig which he would sooner forget, but by which we called him now and then for the fun of it, holding out for free speech and a democratic society in tiny Granville, Illinois. We became friends, and it became clear to each of us, and I guess to many others, that we formed a family. We did things together, we talked together, we ate together, we went to church together, and of course he cut my hair. Julius had adopted us.

In the spring of 1963 Nancy and I wanted to visit Union Seminary and Julius wanted to come. He knew he would enjoy the people and the place; he hoped to meet Reinhold Niebuhr. I promised to try to introduce him. He and I drove out while Nancy flew to Atlanta for a wedding and then on to New York where we met up again. Jules couldn't wait to get started, and we left Granville late on a Sunday night. We stopped at a motel in Indiana for a few hours' sleep, and he had me up at six in the morning, insisting we move out. Somewhere on the Ohio Turnpike while he was driving the speedometer went haywire and began to fluctuate wildly, registering as much as a hundred and twenty miles an hour.

"Look at me," he crowed. "I'm hell on wheels."

He was like a kid going to the circus. We stopped off in Clinton, New Jersey, to see Uncle Rey for a few minutes, and then spent the night with the relatives in Watchung. My mother and father were the only teetotalers in the family, and Julius felt right at home in Watchung, especially with Aunt Helen who kept him liberally supplied with, as he always put it, "booze."

Julius had the time of his life, and in the most unlikely of places: a theological seminary. This man in his early sixties who had largely forsaken the church because he was certain it had forsaken him, loved it all: the meals, both in the seminary refectory and across Broadway at Dottie's diner; living in a dormitory; the nightly bull sessions; and perhaps most of all the daily morning chapel services. He could not get enough of going to church. Here, he said, it was different. He loved the intellectual excitement that hung in the air, and he recognized a depth of commitment and purpose, uniting hearts and minds, he had never felt before. And of course, there was Reinhold Niebuhr.

"Now remember," he prodded, "we must try to see Reinie."

"I know, Jules," I replied, "I'll do my best."

We went to Niebuhr's office and learned that he was seldom there now; he was in virtual retirement though still living at the seminary. And his health had continued to decline. A secretary told us that he was scheduled to deliver a lecture just across the street at Barnard College at three in the afternoon. So off we went, Julius in high spirits, reasonably confident he would now meet the man he had so long admired and so often quoted. We stepped out on the Broadway side of Union and crossed 120th Street walking south. As we approached the entrance to Barnard, I recognized Niebuhr coming toward us. He wore a familiar beret and walked with the limp that had marked him since a stroke. There was no mistaking him.

"There he is now, Jules, right there, coming toward us," I said.

"That's Reinie?" he asked, and then answered himself doubtless recalling a picture of Niebuhr. "Yes, that's Reinie."

"Dr. Niebuhr," I said as we intercepted him, "we were just on our way to hear your lecture at Barnard."

"I'm not lecturing at Barnard," he growled in that singular voice. "I don't know where you got that idea."

I identified myself as a recent Union graduate and said it was fortunate that we had met on the street, as the real purpose of attending the lecture was to introduce him to a friend who had long read and admired him. I presented Julius and they shook hands and chatted while Nancy and I stood by. This was Julius's moment. Then Niebuhr excused himself to continue on his way back toward Union Seminary, the last time I ever saw him. Julius might as well have shaken hands with a choir full of angels. His trip, all of it special, was now crowned with glory. He had met Reinhold Niebuhr, a theologian he could respect and respond to, and the man arguably our most influential intellectual during the second quarter of the twentieth century.

About a year after we had arrived in Granville, Julius said to us quite suddenly one day, as we stood outside our home by the steps, "I'm really going to miss you guys when you leave."

I said we were not then "looking." He knew, though, that ministers move on, and often young ministers move sooner rather than later. I don't know which of us spoke first.

"You can come with us."

That was all. We had not discussed it. We were offering to adopt him.

"That would be great," he said, but he didn't sound convinced. We warmed to it.

"Why not, Jules?" I asked. "It's up to you. You don't have family and obligations here. And you don't plan to stay in the barber shop forever, do you? You really could come with us if you wanted to."

"You're part of our family, Jules," Nancy said. "You know that, don't you?"

"It's not likely to happen," he said, afraid to trust the idea. We could tell he liked it.

That touched off Nancy.

"Now listen, Jules, if I tell you you're part of our family, you are. That's all there is to it. When we leave Granville, you can come with us. We'll count on it."

He seemed to glimpse it as a possibility.

"That would be nice," he said wistfully. "It really would be nice."

"Consider it done," Nancy announced.

Later, alone, she and I reassured each other, and ourselves, that we meant it. When Marjorie was born, we asked Julius to be her godfather. She was a week late in arriving, and Julius had planned a fishing trip. He stalled his companions for a few days, but they finally left on the morning of the day she was born twelve hours later. He promised to call to keep posted on the now imminent birth, and I told him that ten minutes after she came into the world, Margie raised herself up in the delivery room and asked, "Where's Julius?" He loved it. My father baptized her in the Granville church and Julius stood with us for the ceremony. Margie always called him "my godfather."

When we left Granville the following year for Evanston, just over a hundred miles away, Julius wasn't ready to make the move with us. He came up to see us about every six weeks. Our friends became his friends, and I took him over to the university to hear lectures and meet faculty. He liked and was impressed by Robert Wiebe and bought his book *The Search for Order*, which Wiebe graciously inscribed in the spidery hand I had come to know well.

The summer after my mother and father moved to Maine, Julius came out to be with us there at Lake Sebago. He played the skeptic to my father's man of faith, but usually wound up sounding a transcendental note. Because my father had a mystical strain in his make-up, they had a grand time, these two peace-loving spirits, who yet recognized the need for power to redress injustice. They had both read Niebuhr. There on the lake in Maine in the mid-sixties they talked of Martin Luther King, Jr., who also had been influenced by Niebuhr, and whose call to conscience evoked admiration from these two men of conscience. If Julius had a favorite hymn, it was the theme song of the civil rights movement, "We Shall Overcome."

He was approaching seventy and said he'd had enough of the barber shop. He didn't need to work any longer to support himself, and he felt increasingly bored cutting hair. He wanted to get out of the shop, but he didn't want to be left with nothing to do in Granville. What would happen when we left Evanston?

In March of 1971 I was offered a position teaching American history at North Carolina Wesleyan College in Rocky Mount. We planned to move in late July.

"We're going to North Carolina," we told him.

"I'm coming with you," he declared immediately.

"Good," we said.

And he did. But before he left Granville, he suffered a major heart attack. Now he had decided to make the break and come with us, and that speeded his recovery. He promised us he would be there by Labor Day and he was. He rented his house, packed up his Nancy Wilson tapes, threw in his golf clubs, and mounted his Mustang. Julius was seventy when he joined us in the Tar Heel State, and would remain a part of our family until he died nearly four years later. There was nothing legal in the arrangement; everything depended on trust and goodwill. He just moved in with us. We had, in fact, adopted him and he us. He agreed to fund our monthly mortgage payment, and we both came out ahead financially. That more than paid his way with us, but it was less than it would have cost to maintain himself.

He wanted to keep his house in Granville. Despite the act of faith that brought him from Illinois to North Carolina, he felt unsure we would stick to the bargain.

"We're in this together, Jules," we would say. "You're part of our family now, and that's that."

"You don't know," he would reply. "You don't know how you will feel. You may change your mind."

"Even if we do," we would say, "that won't make any difference. It's like being married: you know, for better or worse."

It was a simple commitment for us, one we thought should be self-evident. But he could see that marriages were falling apart with alarming frequency, and maybe our new "marriage" would founder too. We always tried to assure him that however we might fall out with each other, and however hard it might be to make it work, we would not dissolve the understanding. We couldn't. But that is something that must be shared in mind and spirit and experience; a simple declaration won't do. We realized that he would have to live his way, and we with him, into a final confidence.

Our roomy old house allowed him to have an upstairs bedroom with a private bath and a large closet, as well as a porch off the back. The house was ours but the room was his. He always insisted that we were welcome there too. One symbol of this was his purchase of a color TV, which he had installed in his room. It became, to his great satisfaction, a family viewing center, and from sports to drama, we gathered there with him to share it.

Julius and I shared another ritual in his room. He continued to cut my hair after we moved to Rocky Mount, seating me on a stool in his bedroom and plying the tools of his trade as well as ever, if a bit slower. He had tired of being a barber, but he remained committed to "doing it right" when he attended me. Always attentive to appearances, he wanted his shoes well-shined, but it was harder for him to do it as he aged and weakened. We made a bargain. He would cut my hair once a month and I would shine a pair of his shoes once a week. He kept his part of the agreement better than I kept mine.

Julius enjoyed Scotch whiskey. He told us it was an acquired taste, immensely worth cultivating, and we were missing a good thing. He drank moderately, and was never drunk, but he did insist on a daily libation or two. He would have his booze. Usually he indulged in his pleasure in his room, sometimes while he read or watched TV and sometimes while he just sat there in his recliner and pondered and imagined and remembered. He enjoyed drinking company, and almost anyone who liked a drink qualified for his most pronounced ritual. A few months after I began teaching at Wesleyan, I won a half gallon of Seagram's whiskey in a raffle sponsored by the junior class. I gave it to Julius, and it kept him happy for two months.

Nancy would later teach English and Latin at Rocky Mount Senior High, and it seemed quite natural when she was asked to advise the AFS Club for foreign and domestic student exchanges. We hosted first an Italian girl and then a Danish boy in our home. Once when some visiting British friends went grocery shopping, when the girl at the "till" heard the accent she said, "You must be staying with the Joneses." Our friends were astonished and asked how she could know that, not realizing she was Nancy's student. "They do that," she replied.

Our children were born into our friendship with Julius. When we moved to Rocky Mount, Margie was seven, Brooks was four, and Rachel was eighteen months. We nearly always ate supper together, and if neither Nancy nor I could be home at noon, he gave the children lunch. He sometimes took Brooks to the cafe where he liked to drink coffee and loaf, and he told us that our son had never met a stranger. He took them all for rides in his Mustang. Often they would gather up old bread and drive down to the city lake and feed the ducks. Sometimes afterwards he would drive them around, letting them choose which way to turn at each intersection. When they wound up out in the country, as they often did, he would solemnly announce, "we're lost," and they would laugh and squeal and say, "let's get lost some more." They always made it home for supper.

The hardest thing we had to do was tell him, as his health and strength failed, that he must stop taking the children for rides his car. It was no longer safe. Friends confirmed what we had noticed, that he seemed increasingly inattentive when he drove. And so we had to tell him. It hurt us to say it and it hurt him to hear it, but he accepted it without complaining.

Perhaps the most lasting picture we retain of him with one of our children is of his sitting in his recliner watching a golf match on TV, our little Rachel curled up beside him, wide-eyed at this new game which moved so slowly, and yet which so compelled his interest. In the early 1970's Johnny Miller was a big name and money-winner on the PGA circuit.

"Let's go watch Johnny," he would say.

"Let's go watch Johnny," she would repeat.

And they did, he peaceful and content in his chair holding her close, and she charmed by his companionship and secure in his care. We have a picture of Julius and Rachel, when she was still a baby barely able to stand. He is sitting down and she is leaning against him; she looks up into his face with trust and wonder and he looks down at her with a love allowed only to grandparents. It is Ghirlandaio's famous painting of an old man and a child, except that here the old man is not ugly but fine looking.

It worked out remarkably well. As in any close relationship there were tensions and anxieties, but it seemed to us they were always at a minimum. Often when we discussed the arrangement with skeptical people we had to remind them that Julius was not a parent or an uncle, for they would say they didn't think they could manage with their parents. Always we replied that he was not that, but a special friend, and Margie identified him to her friends as her godfather. Most people applauded our effort, though some seemed threatened by it. Our life with Julius set forth a human truth that challenged the anxious privacy of the nuclear family. Nothing meant more to me than my parents' reaction when we told them, "Julius is coming with us." Without hesitating my father said, "that's great," and my mother added, "oh, yes." Adoption seemed a good thing still.

In anything unconventional, critics wait for the slightest mistake, miscue, or misfortune in order to pounce with a mean-spirited "I told you so." Never mind that in the best of families things go wrong and life is never perfect. Those who cannot admit of possibilities such as the one we realized with Julius want them to fail. Sometimes, even when they succeed by any standard, such people still deny the truth before them. One person simply refused to acknowledge that our arrangement was working, and announced that we were deluded to think so. Much more decent was the appreciative attitude of an Evanstonian who commended us for adopting Julius, and said simply he thought himself incapable of such an effort. "I'd grouse about it," he said.

We learned with Julius what everyone needs to know, that all attempts to care and nurture need help. The rearing of children, the sustaining of a marriage, and the encouraging of the aging need more than a direct, however intimate, relationship. We all need a community, and many friends in Rocky Mount helped us provide such a community for Julius. Neighbors and colleagues adopted him too.

He made friends at North Carolina Wesleyan. He had always longed for the college atmosphere he had never enjoyed, and Wesleyan became a second home to him in Rocky Mount, where he stalked the truth he always said could not be found. Yet he pressed on after it. He established himself as a regular in the office of our friend and neighbor, Daisy Thorp, who directed the Upward Bound program housed on campus. A colleague in history recognized in Julius a kindred spirit, and took him along to an evening class he taught in Raleigh. Julius wouldn't have missed it; he even went for the final exam. Another colleague in the religion department was an educational consultant who traveled extensively, and frequently he took Julius with him. Once they spent a week in Caracas at an international conference. All these people gave us enormous credit for adopting Julius, but we felt the credit belonged to them, and others, too. We simply could not have done it alone.

Julius continued to write poetry and won third place in a Wesleyan competition. His twin themes had always been social justice and romantic love. We knew his painful crush on the young English teacher in Granville had inspired a poem. In Evanston he became enamored of a student to whom Nancy and I introduced him. He wrote her a love letter, though she seemed not to notice. Now in Rocky Mount, he felt freer to act on his feelings, especially toward a French teacher who had been a nun and an undergraduate who could never be one. He took them out, usually to dinner. He spruced up and preened like a peacock as he came down from his room to go out to his car and collect his date for the evening. This, obviously, was another source of renewal for him. Externally these friendships were platonic, but we knew that for him they were erotic. He loved our family, he loved Wesleyan College, and he loved women. And they loved him. It gave him spark and purpose and visceral self-esteem.

Each summer he returned to Illinois to play golf with some friends, staying with his wife's sister and her husband. He continued to rent his house. He always returned to Rocky Mount by Labor Day, glad he had gone but happy to be back. He no longer said we might tire of him and want him to leave, but his house in Granville remained a symbol of his lingering uncertainty. Until the last summer of his life. He came back to Rocky Mount in late August to announce that he had decided to sell his house and, laughing, that we were now stuck with him. I slapped him on the back and Nancy hugged him.

He was in good spirits that year, but he had aged noticeably and his health failed rapidly. At Christmas he had a near-fatal heart attack and spent eighteen days in the hospital. The doctors determined he had suffered a "silent heart attack" the previous summer while he was in Illinois. It was now obvious that his heart was damaged and weak. When he came home he could not yet make it to the second floor, and we made our living room into a bedroom for him. He progressed, following his doctor's prescription to climb one step the first day and an additional step each following day. On the sixteenth day he finally arrived triumphant at the top of the stairs. His glory was fleeting. We could see him fail. At times the spark was gone from his spirit and the light was absent from his eye. He sat more now, just sat in his room and depended on people to come to him. The children were wonderful about going in to see him. His color TV was an attraction, but they went to be with him.

In late winter of 1975 we realized he had become especially sensitive to Tiamat, our big Lab, who was also fast declining. She would come up and lie down next to Julius as he sat in his chair watching TV, and he would pet her and just touch her. I think he clung to her as a metaphor of mortality. He knew she was getting old, and he knew his own strength was diminishing. Man and dog knew and comforted each other.

Julius suffered another heart attack on April 1, 1975, and he was not fooling. In great pain he asked us to take him to the hospital. On the way he said, "You guys are finding out about the responsibility of taking care of an old person." We told him we were a family. He was placed immediately in the coronary care unit and given little chance to leave it alive. Early on the first Sunday morning after he had been admitted, the doctor phoned and told us that Julius had at best two hours to live. If we wanted to see him we had better get out there right away.

We had tried to prepare for this, but one is scarcely ready to be told by the attending physician that this is "it." Good old Jules was having none of it. He seemed asleep and looked very pale and weak. When I called his name, he opened his eyes and murmured something by way of acknowledgment. Then he said he was tired. Well, I said, if you're tired, Jules, try to get some rest. Go to sleep. We'll come back later.

"I want one more summer of golf," he declared, eyes closed again, and quite still.

Uncomprehending, I said that was nice, and why didn't he just go to sleep now.

"I want one more summer of golf," he repeated.

"Well, Jules," I said, as we stood by his bed and I leaned over toward him, "if you want to play golf you have to get some rest. You need to build up your strength. You have to sleep."

"Oh, no," he said almost vigorously. "If I go to sleep I won't wake up again. I have to stay awake to play golf." And with that he was asleep again and we came home.

He fooled the doctors for three and a half weeks. In a private room, he had a steady run of visitors, including his brother and his brother-in-law from Illinois, and for a time Nancy and I took turns staying the night with him. After all, the doctors continued to assure us he simply could not last much longer. We did not want him to die alone. He hated being fed intravenously and begged to have the needles removed from his arms. Nancy hit on a pleasurable alternative. He was being fed glucose and water through his veins. Why, she wondered, could he not ingest essentially the same ingredients in a far more enjoyable form, namely Pepsi-Cola. The doctors agreed, out came the tubes, and in went the Pepsi. We bought it in two-liter containers and he drank it continuously until he finally lost consciousness and slipped into a coma, many liters later. Whoever discovered Pepsi, he would say again and again, must have been sick. What a way to ease the pain! Increasingly he needed someone to give it to him, and by the time he died I imagined I had fed him more Pepsi than I had fed food to my three children. It satisfied him unfailingly. He asked for it, he called for it, he demanded it.

Once, thinking he had dozed off, I stepped out in the hall to talk with a nurse. When I returned he was quite annoyed and said loudly, "Pepsi, Pepsi-Cola, for Christ's sake." I gave it to him and apologized for being out of the room when he had wanted a drink. A day or so later when he again seemed to doze, he suddenly called out, "I'm thirsty, I need something to drink."

"Well, how about some Pepsi-Cola, for Christ's sake," I said.

Much of institutional life is not only impersonal but undignified. There was Julius, terminally ill, lying abed in a hospital gown, drifting in and out of consciousness, alternately declaring he wished to die and get it over with and then enjoying another round of Pepsi. Before he died he became incontinent and incoherent, but short of that he made us laugh, stealing the initiative from his circumstance. Anyone who has ever seen an old man move about in a flapping nightgown knows how silly it can look. Open at the back for convenience, it can also be hard on someone who has cared for appearances.

Julius came to the time when he could not make it to the bathroom alone. One of us would help him out of bed and across the floor, then through the bathroom door where he would slowly and uncertainly turn and ease down to the toilet. These things we take for granted most of our lives become paramount when charged with necessity or disability. Julius's safe arrival on the toilet seat was an achievement. Once, settling in with flatulent relief, he declared solemnly, "Lafayette, we are here."

When he could no longer make it to the bathroom, one of us helped him out of bed and onto a portable commode. By now necessity displaced any sense of privacy or modesty. Only relief would do. One reads of people kidnapped by terrorists who are guarded night and day. After awhile, they later report, you lose your sense of modesty. Hospital confinement, though meant to be benign and not malicious, may seem like a terrorist kidnapping to the patient/victim.

I had long thought that life's essential issue remained the same, whatever the context in which it must be faced. The issue was simply this: How do I, how do we, choose; what do we decide? It is easy enough to philosophize about what it means to be human when one is comfortable, secure, well-fed, and the future looks bright. But what really happens under pressure? Do pain and deprivation bend that meaning out of shape, or is the issue constant, whatever the circumstances? With Julius we learned much. His hospitalization both taught us something new and confirmed the idea of an essential humanness.

What we learned was a paradox of weakness and strength. As people become older, and especially as they become infirm and restricted, quite obviously they cannot do what they once could. This is but an accelerated variation on life's theme of slowing down, something everyone experiences who is fortunate enough to live long enough. We lament loss, we bemoan our frailty, we wax nostalgic about the good old days. But just here is a strange thing. Out of increasing powerlessness comes a new power: the power to command. Who can refuse one old or sick? We defer to them. We may take our chances in a conversation of peers, but we quickly relinquish the floor to one in, as somebody so nicely put it, "reclining health." We know we should appear as boors or bullies otherwise. This is not reverence for the wisdom of age, but something quite different. This, we think, is the least we can do.

Power is power, and whenever it is exercised, it can corrupt. When Julius was in the hospital, frustrated by his confinement, he turned that very limitation into an expansion of his control over others by demanding attention on his own terms. Professionals are largely immune to this. But family and friends and sympathetic visitors are wonderfully vulnerable to such manipulation. The very weakness and powerlessness of a patient can produce a tyranny that in the end harms the patient himself more than the person it aims at.

Julius was entrapped, first in his hospital room and then by his bed. He talked his way free of the intravenous tubes but he could not will strength and soundness back into his body. What he could do was demand "Pepsi-Cola, for Christ's sake." That became something of a metaphor. He was increasingly peremptory. Everyone noticed it. At first we marked it up to his physical condition. He was sick and weak, and really knew he was dying. Having wanted one more year of golf, he knew with each passing day that he would not have it. There was, we felt, fear and anxiety in his voice and eyes. We would be understanding above all. Someone is old, someone is sick, someone is dying. What can one do but oblige?

Plenty. One can refuse the temptation to bury the patient before he dies. Julius was not simply reaching out blindly and frantically as he ordered us about to wait on him. He had discovered his final source of worldly power. All else was now gone irretrievably. What remained was the possibility of a tyranny he could never have known earlier. That it was not imagined but real, both for him and for us, was clear one day when I was with him as he dozed off and on. Twice he opened his eyes and asked for Pepsi Cola, which now had to be administered with attention to each detail down to placing the straw in his mouth. He could no longer sit up or raise himself even slightly from the pillow. Each time when I reached him with the drink, he murmured a refusal, closed his eyes, and tightened his mouth. The first time I thought nothing of it, but the second made me wonder. Then he asked again. I let a moment pass before I spoke.

"You know, Jules," I said, "if you keep asking for something when you don't want it, someone may not take you seriously when you really do." I wanted to be gentle but I felt I needed to say it. I was stunned by his response. His voice was strong and his enunciation clear as he said, "Wolf, wolf."

Wolf, wolf. There it was. He knew, and now he knew that I knew. He said it, not I. Wolf, wolf. This was the last game, the final throw, his supreme joke. And always a profound paradox. <u>He knew</u>. He understood the shifting balance of ordinary power and control, and was determined to offset it, and if not that, to slow its rush to overtake him. It was as if he were an army, badly beaten, in retreat, blowing up railroads and bridges to slow the advancing and conquering enemy. He knew. The third time he took the Pepsi when I offered it.

Julius became uncomfortable simply lying there in his bed. After Pepsi Cola, the thing he most immediately appreciated was to have his neck and shoulders massaged. Propped up on pillows, he would lean forward while one of us so ministered to him. "That's it," he would say, "that's it." And often he'd say, "Rub the hell out of it." As he slipped more often in and out of consciousness he became too weak to sit up. Then he would ask to be turned on his side so that someone could rub him. Always he grunted and moaned with pleasure, and it seemed a simple enough thing to do to try to ease the burden of his final struggle. For all our attempts to define and describe the meaning of love, what could mean more to a dying man than to have his back rubbed?

He began to ask us to rub his buttocks; they too were sore. Books on massage make it plain that the buttocks respond indiscriminately to such attention. You can't go wrong; anything feels good. We acted on his pleas to "rub my ass." Early in the week he died I was alone with him, reading while he seemed to doze. Then he said abruptly, "My ass is sore."

"Is it, Jules?" I responded, putting down my book. "Would you like me to rub it?"

"Yeah," he grunted.

"Fine," I said, "I'll turn you over." I stood up and began to move toward him. "Which way do you want to turn?"

It was more like a wail than anything else. "There you go," he said, "picking on me. Sick people can't decide."

"Jules," I said, close to him now, "I'll be happy to rub you. Just tell me which way you'd like to turn."

"You're being mean to me," he said. "You know sick people can't decide. My ass hurts."

"I'm sorry your ass hurts," I said, "but I'm not going to turn you over until you tell me which way."

He blamed me again, muttering an imprecation. This was, it would seem, no time for Pepsi. "Why don't you help me?" he bleated.

"I will," I said. "Just tell me which way you want to turn."

"Ahhhhhh, sick people….. you're mean…. my ass hurts."

It seemed right to me to ask him to make a simple choice. I would be dismissing him to the dead otherwise. Here was life reduced to the irreducible. A man lay nearly helpless in a bed in a hospital, surrounded by institutional devices to "care" for him, and he wanted his bottom rubbed. But he was still a man, still a person, still a human being. He was not past caring and wanting and hurting. And he was not past choosing. I was sure it was right to give the choice, a very simple one, to him. I would not participate in his own self-abnegation. It was more than just giving him the choice; it was necessary to insist that he take it. If he refused, then he denied himself. I would not deny him.

It was easy then and it is easy now to say that in that tiny choice, in that decision to decide which way to be turned in his bed that I might rub his ass, I lacked understanding. Perhaps I did. But the meaning of being human confronted us both in that moment. And that moment in that hospital room confirmed for me what I had long believed, that though circumstances vary radically, the essential issue remains. The escape from freedom can assume large social dimension, it can be presented in powerful literary and dramatic representations, and it tempts each of us, I suspect, every day. Here lay a man, nearing death, as we both knew, but a man. All the more important that he remain a man, to himself and me, precisely because time had almost run out.

When he used the "magic word" that generations of mothers and grandmothers have taught their children, it was hard to hold my ground, but I did. "Please rub my ass," he said, pitifully, beseechingly. "Tell me which way to turn you and I will," I said. He wouldn't and I didn't. Julius went back to sleep.

I told Nancy and Daisy of it, and they agreed, perhaps to encourage and support me. But I think they meant it. Since then we've all reflected on it often as a moment that gathered up much of life's essential meaning. Love does not always mean saying yes; it may require us to say no. My no to Julius was an insistence that he join me in saying yes to himself; that he could not and must not give up. He knew what he was doing in crying "wolf, wolf" when he called for Pepsi. This was another form of manipulation, and a worse one because it debased him even as he sought to use me. It is nice to be able to report that during the next few days he could say decisively which way he wished to be turned that we might massage him.

Two days before he died, Julius became semi-comatose, and he slipped out of English and into Danish. When he was awake he could understand English, but seemed unable any longer to speak it. He babbled and chattered in Danish, only Danish. Knowing nothing of the language, we sought some way to let him know we wanted to be in touch, and hit on the idea of simply saying Danish names and places. "Hans Christian Andersen," I would say, and Julius would respond with a "ja, ja, ja," eyes closed. "Kierkegaard," I would say, and get the same response. He had told us of playing with the future King Christian V as a boy, and so we tried that: "King Christian V." Always the response came back: "ja, ja, ja," in a descending inflection. We tried "Copenhagen" and "Bornholm," the island of his birth and youth. It never failed. It seemed not to matter how often we repeated these few names. It became as a responsive litany.

Julius died on a Saturday about supper time. He went into a coma the evening before. My last exchange with him came on Friday, just after noon. His eyes were closed, as they had been, and he remained "in Danish" when he tried to speak. I was about to leave, having spent the latter part of the morning with him. Nancy had come to relieve me and sit with him. She went to him and took his hand and told him she was there, and I got up to leave. Then I sat down again by his bed and said, "All right, Jules, we're going sing "We Shall Overcome". I set the pitch and he joined in on it, never missing a note, not garbling a single word. In English. He never opened his eyes. I patted his hand as I got up, looking at Nancy, and left. That evening when we arrived he was comatose, and he died the next day.

What was his legacy? As much as anything it was that last and final effort to communicate, and more than that to join his adoptive couple in a singing testimony to social conviction, personal confidence, and perhaps even ultimate hope. He made our family better, and told us and anyone else who will listen the truth about adoption. "I've had three families," he liked to say: "One by birth, one by marriage, and one by love."

A Circumstance for Praise

"You may amount to something someday, Rachel," I said, patting her arm and laughing.

It was the summer before my father died, and we had finished supper in their house on the lake in Maine.

"You certainly turned out to be worth the ten dollars we paid for you," said my mother, and my father added, "in a basket."

"What do you mean?"

"Why, that's what we paid for you," said my mother, "that was the whole cost of your adoption. We got you for ten dollars, including the lawyer's fee. And you came in a basket. You were ten days old."

"Ah, Dad," said Brooks, "you were a basket case when you were still a baby."

Everybody loved it, especially his grandfather, who said, "You have to get up early in the morning to keep ahead of Brooks." The grandson was quite pleased.

"I remember hearing about being ten days old," I said, "but what is this about ten dollars and a basket?"

"Didn't we ever tell you this story?" inquired my father in a tone that assumed they had, long since. Nothing had been intentionally concealed. They simply had never told me. I would have remembered the basket.

"Well," picked up my mother, "there was a lawyer who knew we wanted a baby and so he arranged it. He knew a doctor there in Braselton and he told him about our wanting a baby. The doctor said he would let the lawyer know when he learned of a baby for adoption. And he did. He made all the arrangements, and the entire cost, including his fee, was ten dollars. You were a ten-dollar baby." She laughed and said, "And you've been worth it."

"Yes," my father put in, "we sure got our money's worth out of that investment."

My mother was leaning forward with her arms on the table, and had upon her face that expression which so often marked her when she spoke of something too good to be true. My father leaned back in his chair, smiling and content, as he did when the world seemed right. It was right for him now, in the evening of his life and closer to night than we could know. Here was his family which meant so much to him. He loved being with us, and hearing and seeing us be with each other.

"And you came in a basket," he said.

"Oh, yes," said my mother excitedly, "in a basket. Oh, you were so cute. It was out in the country away from town, so nobody else would be likely to see what was taking place. The arrangement was that the lawyer would meet your mother ten minutes before we were to arrive, and she would give the baby—that's you—to him, and then he would give the baby to us. It was all worked out, down to a schedule."

I was hooked on the story, but felt odd at hearing my mother refer to the woman who bore me and was now giving me up for adoption as my "mother."

"Yes," said my father, "yes, that's right. But we couldn't wait. We were so anxious to see you that we jumped the gun on our end of the bargain. We got there ten minutes early."

"Oh, yes," said my mother, now alternating with my father in telling the story, as easily and confidently as if they were delivering dialogue on stage, and perhaps even more resembling a liturgical ritual. "Oh, yes, we knew we were supposed to arrive ten minutes later, that we were supposed to wait until your mother handed you over to the lawyer, but we just couldn't. Daddy Alan was so excited, he just had to see his new baby."

"You were excited too, Mother," said my father.

"So what happened after you got there?"

"We drove our old car out there ahead of time," my father continued, "and parked up on a little hill in the road, so we could try to see what went on."

"Could they see you?" I asked.

"I don't know," said my father. "We tried to stay out of sight."

"The lawyer was already there in his car when we got there," my mother said, "and we saw the other car drive up, and your mother got out. I'm sure that's who it was. I don't know who was driving the car, probably her mother. She got out with you in the basket."

"What kind of basket?" one of the children wanted to know.

"Like a laundry basket," said my mother. "You were in a laundry basket, and she handed you over to the lawyer. Oh, we were so excited, we couldn't wait to get down there. But of course we had to wait until your mother left. We didn't want to cause any embarrassment."

"We didn't have to wait long," said my father. "She gave you to the lawyer and then turned around and went back to her own car, and drove away. I'm sure she hated to give you up. We couldn't hear anything from where we were, but when we got down there the lawyer told us that after he took the basket from her, she looked down at you in it and said, 'Be a good boy.'"

It went right through me. I think it touched everyone else too.

"I've tried to do that," I said, "though it's a pretty big assignment." I spoke very quickly because I did not trust silence.

"Yeah, Dad," said Brooks, "too big for you."

Everybody laughed, and my mother came to my defense.

"Oh, you were a good boy, you've always been a good boy," she said in her characteristically sweet and understanding way.

"But you're still a basket case, Dad," said Brooks, smiling as he does when he works a put-down.

"Once we had you in that basket," said my mother, "you were ours, and we were so happy to have you."

"Yes," said my father, "and do you remember how you took him straight up to New Jersey? You didn't even go back to our house."

"You didn't take me home?"

"That's right. We were in rural Georgia, and we wanted to be sure you were all right, so I took you straight up to New Jersey to have you checked by a pediatrician, and to visit with my family. As soon as we had you in the car, we drove to the station in Winder, and I took you on the train to New Jersey."

"You took me to New Jersey from Georgia before you even took me to your house?"

"That's right. Daddy Alan drove me to the station with you on my lap in your basket, and I took you to New Jersey and he went back home."

"So I got out of Georgia at a very young age," I said laughing. "I've heard about the trip north on the train, but I had no idea it was the day of my adoption."

"The very hour," said my mother, altogether engaged in reconstructing the event, as my father remained contentedly presiding over his family at his table. "Oh, it was exciting." And then she laughed too. "There you were, a brand new baby, and I had no experience with a baby, but I was taking you all the way up to New Jersey. You didn't seem worried, how could you be? But I was anxious all the way, afraid something might happen to you. There was a very nice conductor who helped me heat your bottle. And when we got to Newark, I was glad to see Helen and Lucy, and I guess mother was there too, and little George, and so proud to show you to them. But mostly I was relieved. Helen rushed right up and said, 'Now Carol, don't worry about a thing. I'll take him to my pediatrician and I'll take care of all the expenses.' Of course we didn't have any money, and she knew that. Helen has always been a wonderful sister."

It seemed strange that my father had been so eager to "get" me, and apparently so willing to relinquish me immediately to the ministrations of the relatives on my mother's side. But then Daddy Alan was always something of a puzzle. It was the image of a baby in a basket that fixed my attention and my imagination. It often has been remarked that people picture themselves after they are dead, laid out in a casket, perhaps viewed by others. Here I had a very different vision, of myself laid out in a basket at the beginning of my life. While I had to create the figure of the woman who brought me to the lawyer, and the lawyer himself, because I had seen my own baby pictures I had a clear image of myself lying there as the woman gave me to the lawyer, and he, in turn, passed me on to my mother and father. From my earliest memory I had known of the adoption, and where I had been born to a single young woman whom I presumed to be a nearby Georgian. My mother and father never sought to deceive me about my earthly origin, and so delivered me from that burden so many adopted people feel. They were my parents and I was their son, and that was that. I was born, and then at ten days they made me theirs. But the transaction was invisible and abstract. The story of how it actually happened, and particularly the basket, furnished a visual specificity that fascinated me. Nancy and the children loved it, and I knew Daisy Thorp would too.

When we returned to North Carolina, I went up to her house to tell the tale. Our good friend and neighbor, she was my faculty colleague at Wesleyan, chairing the art department. She knew my mother and father.

"There is something I must tell you," I said, "something that you'll love."

"Tell, tell," she said, as she always did in such a moment.

"It's about my adoption, about how Mama Carol and Daddy Alan actually got me."

"Oh, I can't wait. Tell me now."

I sat down at her breakfast table and told her. I knew she would love it all, but especially the basket. That would strike her as esthetically fitting. Nothing would need to be explained. And I knew what would happen when I told her what the woman said to the lawyer. It did. When I repeated what my father had told me, that the woman, as she handed me over in my basket to the lawyer, looked down at me and said, "Be a good boy," Daisy was stricken with the poignancy of it and cried.

"Oh," she said, "oh, how wonderful."

"I knew you'd love it," I said.

"Oh, 'Be a good boy,' oh."

"Yeah, that got me too."

"Did you have your mama write all this down?"

"No, I didn't think of it."

"You must, you must have her write it down."

"You're right. The next time we talk by phone I'll ask her to do that."

"Oh, imagine what that woman must have felt."

For the first time, incredibly, I saw it all differently and realized there was another human being who had a right to some feelings about my adoption. Never before, <u>never</u>, had it crossed my mind that the woman who bore me and gave me up might have let me go reluctantly, much less that she might have missed me. "Be a good boy" had meant to me, when my mother and father told me of it at the table that day in Maine, only that I was being wished well on life's journey, the way a good sport wishes an opponent well before a game. I had always thought of my adoption from our side, my mother's and father's and mine, and never from the woman's who gave me up. Never. There was no curiosity about her, none. And now, telling Daisy the story of my delivery in a basket, brought an understanding from her that jarred me. I always thought of my birth as a problem for my bearer and an opportunity for my mother and father, both resolved by the adoption. Until the story of the basket I had never even tried to imagine what that young woman looked like. She was such an abstraction to me that I somehow saw her frozen in time at the age when I was born. Now I was being asked to consider her as a person, and more than just a human being, a mother. I could not think of her as my mother, except in that irreducibly biological sense I had always been aware of. But Daisy was now telling me, as a mother herself, how anguished another mother must feel to let go of her own child. I still needed a moment to try to get it straight.

"How do you mean?" I asked.

"Oh," she said, "giving up her own child, the baby she brought into the world. Oh, it's so wonderful but so heart-rending that she would say 'be a good boy.' Think of all the times she must have wondered how you turned out, her own baby."

"You know," I said, "I never thought of it, I just never thought of it."

She couldn't believe it.

"You never thought about your own mother?" and already I was cutting her off.

"You know I've always thought of Mama Carol as my mother. Of course I've never thought of," and I paused a bit, "anyone else as my mother."

"Well, I understand that, but I mean now your birth mother," and that did seem a good way to say it, accurate and acceptable.

"No, I never have thought about it, not until just now."

"You never thought about how your mama, I mean your birth mama, might wonder about you and miss you?"

"No, I never have, not until now. It just never occurred to me."

"Being a mother myself makes a difference."

"Yes, I'm sure it does. I can see that."

"Haven't you thought about her, about what's happened to her? Do you have anyway of knowing whether she's still alive? How old would she be now?"

Again, incredibly, I had to realize for the first time I was being brought from an abstraction to a consideration of another human being. A woman became pregnant, bore a child, and because Alan and Carol Jones adopted that child, it became me. It had always been that simple. I never imagined I owed anything to "the other woman." Why should I? I owed every thing to my mother and father. Didn't I?

"No," I said again, "I've never thought about it. When my father used to refer to her as 'your mother,' I thought only of the fact of my birth. That was it, and nothing more. The fact of my birth."

"Don't you wonder what might have become of <u>her</u>? You <u>know</u> she wonders that about <u>you</u>."

Then with that romantic imagination so quick to invent Victorian scenarios, Daisy constructed another one.

"Wouldn't it be wonderful if she could see you now, all grown up and married with children of your own. She must have wondered what you'd look like, and you know she'd be pleased."

"I've never had any desire to search her out," I said. "I've told you that. But you <u>have</u> made me realize something I hadn't thought about before. I really assumed, I guess, that just as I put her behind me, she would put me behind her."

"Oh, no, David, <u>never</u>. Not a mother and her own child. She bore you and there's no way a mother can just put that out of her mind. I <u>know</u> she's wondered about you and missed you through the years. You don't know what's become of her?"

I'm sure I was too short with her this time.

"Of course I don't know. I've told you, I don't know anything about it, except what Mama Carol and Daddy Alan have told me." Then I told her what in fact had conditioned any thought I had ever given to her.

"This may sound odd to you," I said, "but it's a bit like the memory we have of John Kennedy. You know he'll always be young to us, never old, because he's fixed in our minds as he was when he was killed. In some strange way that is how I've thought of her, if at all: Someone fixed in my mind as she was. Only the fixed image was an abstraction, and it wasn't her death but my birth which stopped time. That's how I thought of it."

I realized that even now as I spoke, I had said "it" and not "her." And I began to realize how enormous was my refusal to consider her as a human being. It was one thing to be unallied with those who sought, from curiosity or out of desperation, for their "true parents," their "real mother and father." It was another to freeze in time the one who brought me into my own time's beginning.

"Let's see," said Daisy, "how old would she be if she's still alive? She might be, after all. How old are you?"

"Forty-six," I said.

"And she was probably only sixteen or eighteen when she had you."

I didn't like "when she had you." For me it had always been "when I was born." But this was Daisy the mother talking.

"I think she was probably a little older," I said, "at least twenty. The one thing Daddy Alan told me, more than once, was that she was a college girl. That's how he used to put it: 'your mother was a college girl.' But I guess you're right, she could have been in college and still only eighteen or so when I was born."

"All right," said Daisy, off and running now with this new enterprise, "if you're forty-six and she was eighteen, or even twenty when she had you, how old would that make her now? Now how much older am I than you?"

This was funny to me, and I laughed.

"Twelve years," I said. "I'm forty-six and you're fifty-eight."

"Well, if I'm twelve years older than you are," she announced with renewed confidence, "she would have to be older than I am."

"She would be," I said, "in her mid-sixties, give or take a year or so."

"Who do we know at that age? Maybe she looks like someone we know."

"Hell, Daisy, I don't know," I said, and I thought of Cal Trask in John Steinbeck's *East of Eden*, discovering his mother after all those years of growing up without her, and having, when he finally did come upon her, to make out her features through the darkness of the room in which she sat. I often mentioned literary allusions to Nancy or Daisy when we talked, but I kept this one to myself.

"She's older than I am," she said, "but younger than your mama."

"It's interesting to think of it that way," I said. "There's really a generation's difference between the two if my birth mother was about eighteen or twenty. Mama Carol was thirty-eight when they adopted me."

"What do you think she looks like, and what sort of life do you think she's had?"

"I told you, I haven't thought about it, I really haven't." And then I laughed and said, "If she'd kept me I'd probably have risen rapidly in the Ku Klux Klan."

"Oh, she wouldn't have let you do that," said Daisy. "Why would you say such a thing?"

"Rural Georgia, Daisy, rural Georgia in the thirties and forties and fifties."

"Oh, I see what you mean. But don't you wonder how she's been and what she looks like?"

I spoke very deliberately.

"I've told you that I never gave it a thought, and I suppose I should say a conscious thought, to it. Now I <u>am</u> trying to imagine this woman who was forever the age at which she bore me, in my mind, alive and having lived a life of her own. I suppose she married, but who knows; and I can't imagine what she's done with her life. The chances are, it's been pretty conventional."

"If she married," said Daisy, "she probably had other children. You probably have some brothers and sisters, that is half-brothers and sisters, somewhere. Did you ever wonder about that?"

"No, again it's no," I said. "None of this ever occurred to me before the story of the basket and this conversation with you."

"Oh, the basket," she said. "You really must ask your mother to write all that down."

"I will."

And I did. When we talked by phone a few days later, I asked my mother if she would try to put it all in a letter, and she said she would be glad to.

"Did we tell you what your mother said?" asked my father over the phone, apparently having forgotten that he had, or perhaps wanting to recall it again. "When she gave you to the lawyer and he held the basket with you in it, she looked down at you and said, 'Be a good boy.'"

"Yes, you did tell me that."

Then he told me something he had not said before. My father spoke gently and with much feeling.

"She loved you, Dave."

It all came clear, from the first time he had told me I was adopted to the moment in Maine by the lake a couple of summers before when we sat watching the sun set across Sebago, and talked in the gathering darkness. He had said, "Maybe we didn't do the right thing for you," and paused, and then went on, "maybe we should have tried to find out something about your father." For a moment I had been stunned, and then I knew I was learning something about him and not something about me, and I said urgently, "You're my father," and after another ever-so-slight silence, he had replied, "Thank you, Davey, thank you, Davey Boy." Only then had I realized that he had borne the burden of the adoption, a burden I had not felt. I had never known that earlier, and perhaps he had not felt it much, or at least had not felt compelled to let me know. Maybe it was that his own life was winding down, as it must at his age with his history of rheumatic fever and a weak heart and now the necessary winters in Florida. And so I simply told the truth, that he was my father, my truth and the world's, and saying it I hoped he would feel reassured. He was. Now, on the phone, I knew it was not enough.

"She loved you, Dave."

"Oh, yes, Dear," said my mother, "she must have."

"Look," I said, "I really would appreciate it if you'd write down this account you've given me. Now did I get it right, when we talked at your house when we were there, that you took me right away to catch a train to New Jersey and didn't even go home first?"

"Oh, yes," she said, "and I think the woman I saw there at the other end of the platform was your mother, but of course I didn't want to embarrass her and so of course I didn't ask. She was going one way and I was going the other, up to New Jersey with you."

She hadn't mentioned anything about "my mother" at the railroad station. It was starting to sound like a melodrama.

"Do put it all in the letter," I said. "I'd really appreciate it."

I knew Daisy would catch her breath when I told her what my father had said. I repeated it as he had told it to me, and paused at just the right place for effect and then said it to her.

"She loved you, Dave."

I thought her face would fall apart.

My mother's letter came soon enough, and it was all there, including the part about her waiting for the train in Winder, Georgia, and imagining that she saw the woman from whom I came. It was good to have the letter, a testimony and a purchase on remembrance. Now, I felt, the story is complete, so far as a human story ever is.

Of course it wasn't, as it never is, just when you think it must be.

Two years before he died, my father landed in the coronary-care unit of the hospital in Rocky Mount during the annual stopover on the way south. He recovered sufficiently to make the trip just after Christmas, but I drove them down. He was confident that if he could just reach Florida's friendly climate, he could manage. He did for two more years, doing all the driving himself. But in late January of 1984, he collapsed in church one Sunday morning, and was in and out of the hospital for ten days, and died there on February 8. We talked often by phone, when he was at their winter home and when he was abed in the hospital.

Two days before he died, my mother became quite concerned that his end might be near, and phoned us frequently. She began to worry about the arrangements to be made upon his death. I reminded her that they both had decided to be cremated, and that simplified things. And then I asked if she would like me to come down. Nancy and I had already decided that I needed to go by the next weekend, but now it seemed more urgent.

"Oh, yes, Dear, could you do that? That would mean so much to me. And to Dad."

I assured her I would come, and would plan to arrive on Wednesday, February 8, on a late-afternoon plane. She said a good friend, a German who had come to the United States a few years earlier, could bring her to the airport to meet me. I called my father, back in the hospital at this point, and spoke with him briefly. He was tired and weak and not up to a lengthy conversation, but we were in touch. That was Monday. On Tuesday, I taught an evening course in Raleigh, and did not speak with him, but Nancy told me when I got home that she and Rachel had phoned him and had a good talk. He seemed more rested than he had the day before, and happy to visit with them. He had, he told them, enjoyed the taste of tomato soup. Nancy said she was glad I was going the next day because she did not think he could last much longer. My mother had told him I was coming and that pleased him. Early the next morning she called to tell us he had died in the night. There was nothing to do but go as I had planned; Nancy would come on a later plane. I recalled how he used to tell me that "nobody ever died in his sleep," and realized once more that life is nothing if not ironic. I never second-guessed myself for waiting an extra day. I did what I thought was best, my mother was relieved that I planned to come, and my father was pleased to know I was coming. He never knew I did not get there to see him alive.

He had been home from the hospital briefly on the previous weekend, and on Saturday he and I had had a good talk by telephone. He was relaxed and reflective, openly expressing his gratitude and appreciation for our family, telling me how good it had been together, and thanking me for the joy and delight he had found in Nancy and our children. He was setting the record straight, making ready for the last great adventure. I could hear it in his voice, calm and satisfied.

His fight was over, and he knew it, though he did not say so. He didn't have to. Whatever tension and ambivalence he may have felt was resolved. I could hear that too. His warfare had ended. It was marvelous. We both knew that he was too old and weak to get well again, and we both knew that now it didn't matter. He needed to say one final thing.

"I'm afraid I've been too hard on you."

He said it sweetly, without faltering. He said it as if he really meant it and that somehow it hadn't mattered, that I had turned out all right both because and in spite of him. I had, he may as well have said, been the good boy my birth mother had told me to be when she handed me over in the basket. I felt no resistance to him, no unresolved tension, no abiding dissatisfaction. We were at peace with each other, as he sounded at peace with himself and the world. And the world to come.

"No," I said, "I don't feel that. I think it has all worked out very well."

I meant it. Of course we had had our disagreements and misunderstandings and disappointments. Anything else would be fanciful. But none of that lingered now, none of it claimed my memory or attention. Whatever grief I would feel and whatever mourning I would know, it would not be complicated by unresolved ambivalence or anxiety between us. He had run his race and miraculously hung on into his ninth decade, defying all odds and expectations. He was blessing me as I continued on my own, blessing me and my wife and our children.

"That's nice of you to say," he said, in the same sweet and peaceful tone. Then he called me by the name he had always used when he spoke most affectionately. "Thank you, Davey Boy."

That was how it came to its final fullness between us, the life and love of father and son, begun when he and my mother, in a little Georgia town in a hot summer month, "picked me out."

George was scarcely surprised when I called to tell him.

"We've got to stick together, George," I said impulsively.

"We will," he answered.

And then I said something I had never before declared to him.

"I love you, George."

"Thanks. Dave," he replied. Then he said something he had never said. "I love you, Brother."

There was nothing more to say.

When I went to Florida to collect my mother, I brought back my father's ashes. The idea of cremation arouses neither curiosity nor anxiety in me. But the simple act of seeing and picking up, easily and casually, a cardboard container the size of a shoe box, struck me as comic. We had been through it with Julius, and had felt odd when a child lifted the top from the pottery cookie jar in which we had placed his ashes for burial. Don't let Julius blow away, after all. How absurd to pick up, like any small package, one's own father now mortally reduced to less than a cubic foot of ash.

As we drove, my mother told me that toward the end of his life my father had begun to swear when he felt frustrated. Especially when he made a mistake on his typewriter. It was pretty tame. He would say "hell" or "damn," she told me, but even that was something he never said in my hearing. It had always been "sugar" or "darn it," nothing more. His brothers would have loved it, and maybe some parishioners too. A doctor had discovered Parkinson's disease during a physical; perhaps that was working on him as he typed. I thought it was grand that he could finally let loose and cuss a little since he seemed to want to and, therefore, it must have made him feel better. He had told me two years before he died, as I drove him and my mother to Florida, that he found it harder and harder to pray. Perhaps he had learned a new way to do it. There is always a thin line between prayer and profanity.

We talked of when we had lived and worked and laughed together as a family, mostly at Merom while I was growing up. My mother recalled, ruefully, the night I went away to college, and said she had always been sorry that she and my father went to bed before I left the house. She had not mentioned it before, and he never did.

Driving up through Georgia, I was drawn again back into the past, to the story of my adoption and the laundry basket. I was most intrigued by the possibility that my mother had seen the woman from whom she and my father had just "got me," when she and I waited for the train at the Winder station.

"Why would she be there?" I wondered.

"Well, Dear, because she was going back home, which was the other direction from where I was taking you, up to New Jersey."

"But I don't understand, if she came in a car with me in the basket, why she would head for a train. I mean, didn't she live right around there?"

"Oh, no, Dear, she came from Alabama, you see. She was going back home to Alabama."

"Alabama," I said, surprised, "What do you mean Alabama?"

"Oh, yes, Dear, she was from Alabama, you know, and she would be taking the train back home."

"Nobody ever mentioned that to me. All I ever heard was Hoschton, Georgia, and Braselton. Where did you get the idea about Alabama?"

"Well," she said, moving easily now into a reconstruction of the event, "from the doctor there in Braselton, from his wife. She and I were good friends, you see, when Dad was the minister and her husband was the doctor there. I think she must have told me. She was bored there, you know, living in that little town, and not very happy in her marriage. There wasn't much to do in Braselton, and I think she got bored just playing cards. And it was not a very satisfactory marriage. Her husband was quite interested in sexual experimentation, trying out new things with her."

I was astonished to hear my mother talk of "sexual experimentation." She made a number of references to sex on the trip, but it seemed clear that if the doctor's wife had told her about that, she could have easily revealed some professional confidences as well, namely that the woman who came to the Hoschton clinic to have her baby was not from Georgia but Alabama.

"Why would she come over to Georgia to have a baby if she was from Alabama?" I asked. "Why didn't she stay in Alabama?"

"Well, to protect her reputation and avoid embarrassment. You see, back then, that sort of thing was not looked upon with approval. I think she was a music teacher somewhere in Alabama, and she came over to Georgia to have her baby."

This too was new. My father had said, "Your mother was a college girl," and I had always taken that to mean that she had become pregnant as a student, probably at a nearby Georgia college. Here was my mother saying that the woman in question was a college graduate who had begun a career as a music teacher and then found her life complicated by me.

"How did you learn all this, about being a music teacher, I mean?"

"Oh, from the doctor's wife."

"Well, the important thing is that you and Daddy Alan were there when she was ready to give me up."

"Oh, yes, Dear, that's the important thing. And oh, how glad we've always been. Daddy Alan always thought that was the best thing we ever did, and so do I."

"Thank you, Mama Carol, I'm glad you feel that way," I said, and drove on toward Rocky Mount.

My mother and father had decided that their ashes should be buried in a family repository at the church in Watchung, New Jersey, where she had grown up and where they had been married. An advantage of cremation is that the family is free to choose a time for burial; there is no necessity to get the body in the ground. A disadvantage is that later rather than sooner it may be harder to gather the family together. The earliest time we could plan a committal service for my father's ashes was late June, when Brooks and Rachel were away at camp. George planned a reunion around it, and made the arrangements at the church.

"Dave," he told me, "I checked the pot and there's only room for a handful or two of Alan's ashes."

The ordering of ashes in the family space had been resolved by mixing them in a common container. My father's would be the eighth, as we added him into Grandma and Grandpa Hughes, Lucy and Ernie, Pat's mother and father, and George's father. I said that was fine; we wanted to scatter some up on the old farm and at the home in Maine. The service was brief.

We went back to George and Pat's for lunch and a chance to visit. Having eaten, I moved over to another picnic table, at the edge of the patio and the party, to talk with Squeak. I had finished eating and he wasn't having any. We sat on benches, just the two of us, across the picnic table, the way card players face each other, and leaned into our conversation. It went on for an hour.

I listened to him reminisce, and learned that my father had hung that nickname on him when they were both students at Clinton High School. Squeak said that as they rode the tiny narrow gauge train together for the first time on the way to high school, when Dad was a senior and Squeak was a first-day freshman, someone asked who Casey's companion was. According to Squeak, my father said, "This is my kid brother Squeak. We call him after the family cat." And so it was ever after. Regularly Squeak interrupted himself to say, "This is your heritage, Dave, this is your heritage. You need to know this." His enthusiasm for calling up the past seemed to grow until it became a passion to put everything in order and get it straight, as if we might never have another chance. And always the refrain, "This is your heritage, Dave, this is your heritage."

Squeak recalled how hard the boys had had to work on the farm, and how they were always conscious of debts and interest payments on a mortgage. I said I thought that early experience had conditioned my father decisively, that I could not remember his ever buying anything on time or committing himself to pay for something in the future. He had a very simple view of sound personal economy: buy only what you need and what you can pay for. I kept it up, and said I was glad that my mother and father could afford to do some things as they got older that they obviously enjoyed, such as phoning us now and then. For years he would only write, and then sometimes a postcard. It was cheaper. Such was my impression of the influence upon him of his early experience.

"Dave," said squeak, "let me tell you something. Casey was tight. He was tight, that's all."

I thought of those weekly trips to the post office in Putney, Vermont, when a dollar of my father's salary went into savings for my future education. I thought of his genuine indifference to birthday and Christmas presents for himself, but his concern always to "get me something nice." I remembered his willingness to scrape together everything to send me to college. I thought of Squeak's own recollection of life on the farm. It seemed easily explained and quite unselfish.

"Well," I said, "it's true he was <u>careful</u> with his money, but he always had to be. Don't you think it all goes back to...."

"No, Dave, I'm telling you, Casey was tight. He was just tight, that's all."

I sensed no malice, no desire to levy a late claim against the dead, only a firm conviction born of a direct experience denied me.

"You don't mean you think he was selfish," I asked.

"He was tight, that's all, just tight. Hell, ask Moon." And with that he moved on to other matters called up from memory, including an affectionate account of the high-school basketball team on which my father played. "They were good, Dave," said Squeak. "Clinton was just a little high school, but all over southern New Jersey they were known as the 'fighting five,' and your father was a charter member of that team." To speak of him as a "charter member" was to sanctify him. My father once told me that among all the things he regretted as a youth, the one that haunted him longest was "the time I took a poke at my brother Squeak, because I was older and bigger and thought I could get away with it." Squeak never brought that up to me. My father never forgot it. "It was years," he said to me when I was growing up, and he was trying to teach me from his own experience, "before my brother Squeak forgave me."

I did ask Moon, the nickname Squeak always called Rey by. Was Squeak right? Was Casey tight? Hadn't he simply learned the hard way growing up that debt is bad and in no way worth the illusion of well-being it promises?

"Well," said Rey, "wherever he got it, he got it. He was tight. Now I'm not criticizing, you understand, but Squeak's got a point there. Yes, I'd have to say that Casey kept a pretty tight watch on his money." He recalled spending a considerable time tracking down, at my father's request, a birth certificate in Newark, for which he paid a two-dollar fee. Rey said that my father thought he was kidding when he asked to be reimbursed. "You're really serious about this two dollars?" he asked. "Hell, yes," recalled Rey. "I spent my time tracking this thing down. The least you can do is pay the two bucks." He laughed all the while he told me.

People finally went home as they must, even when they haven't been together since the last funeral and won't be again until the next. Rey and Carolyn drove back to their house near Quakertown, just up the hill from the farm where the boys grew up. I told him, as he left, that we would be up shortly to scatter some of my father's ashes on the old place.

Squeak and Marguerite and Bernice, Arthur's widow, were the last to go. I took the box with the remaining ashes, and we prepared to drive up to Rey's. My mother wanted to come, quite pleased that we would leave some of my father's ashes where he had lived and worked while he went to high school. It was an easy drive of half an hour, and Rey and Carolyn got in with us as we eased down the quarter of a mile to the old driveway, and then drove back along the lane where he had lived and I had played, and Whitey and Barney had demanded of Grandfather Jones, "Come on, Albert, get to work."

We stopped just past where the house had stood. It had long since disappeared, as had the barn where he had sometimes slept when it rained. But the old path away from the house and past the barn, where he had worked and run so often, endured as of the very earth, and here we spread the ashes—Margie, Nancy, my mother, and I. As I let go a handful of ashes, I thought of Loren Eisley's dedication in *The Immense Journey*. It was to his father, he wrote, who lies beneath the prairie and is not forgotten by his son.

What is the measure of a man's life? Not a box of ashes. Wonderful letters of sympathy and appreciation made of my father's death what his whole life had been, what Stanley Romaine Hopper called W. H. Auden's poetry: "a circumstance for praise." Nita Groothuis said simply that she adored him. John Bennett, my father's own model of a Christian scholar, called him a beautiful person. Nick Johnston wrote magnificently of his own years at Merom and of what my father had meant to the shape of his life. For Phil and Mary Sivert he <u>was</u> Merom. Burnie Jarman sent a lovely note, attributing to him "quiet courage" and saying "what a legacy to leave his son." Paul Lynn, a seminary classmate, mourned him as "the gentle poet, who saw goodness and beauty everywhere." Leon Sandborn, his seminary roommate, called him "a rare and beautiful and completely Christian person whom to know was to love, who saw and lived the truth he found in Christ, and applied it to all life—and kept growing in it." Bud Walker may have said it best when he allowed that Daddy Alan "was a Quaker hiding out in the UCC."

My mother wanted to try to make a go of it on her own in the house in Maine where she had been since April, and after the service and visit in Watchung I drove her back up there. Family and friends were in and out much of the summer, especially for a memorial service for my father at the North Windham Union Church, where my cousin George sat behind Nancy and me and our children, and sang "For All the Saints" so triumphantly that the most ardent skeptic might have felt a change of heart. My mother loved having us there, and everyone who came encouraged her to face the future bravely and confidently, but by late July she decided the house was too much for her and that she would be too far from us. She made the decision and we made the arrangements. She would live in an apartment in a newly opened retirement center in Rocky Mount. Early in August as she and I ate supper in the dining room there in the house by the lake, we talked of her move to Rocky Mount.

"You know," she said, "Dad and I were very much in love, so people have trouble understanding how I could actually feel liberated." That was her word; I could not remember hearing her use it before. "But I do," she went on, now eighty-five years old, "and I look forward to being in my home, my place, where I can do what I want when I want."

"That's good," I said, and she went on to tell me of some photographs she had come upon.

"I'm rather surprised," she said, "to find how often in pictures of us Dad is in front of me and I'm back of him or behind him, or peering around him or through his elbow."

"That's very symbolic," I said, "isn't it?"

"Oh, yes," she said, "it couldn't have been otherwise with our personalities."

"It's good you see that," I said. "That's the way it was, and I always thought you were happy with it. But it's important to know it."

"Oh, yes," she said, "I was very happy that way. I always believed in him, but now I have a new life."

I wanted the furnace cleaned before we left for Rocky Mount, and a man came out from Rich's in North Windham. He went down to the basement, detached the part he needed from the furnace, and took it out to his truck. I stood talking to him while he worked on it. As he worked and we talked, a calico cat my mother had befriended jumped up by the repairman. She nestled, purring and importuning, against his side, and he gently brushed her back to the ground.

"You don't want to be up here, you'd get all black," he said.

I told him it wasn't really my mother's but that she fed her and the kitty knew a good thing.

"Sort of like she adopted her," he said.

"Exactly," I said, "sort of like she adopted her."

"And the kitty adopted her too," he added, working on the furnace part.

"And the kitty adopted her too," I repeated.

Epilogue

In "Chariots of Fire" we watch Harold Abrahams, an English Jew, dress for his supreme competitive moment, run the race of his life, and become the world Olympic champion. Sam Mussabini, his half Arab and part Italian running coach, sees none of this. He is in a room from which he can see the stadium, but he will not watch the race and can only wait for the raising of the flag and the playing of the national anthem that will signify the winner. After the race we see Sam in his room, nervously awaiting the result. When he hears "God Save the King" and sees the Union Jack rise above the stadium, he fills with emotion, sits down on the small bed in the modest room, and with tears in his eyes says, "Harold." He smashes his hand through his summer straw hat in speechless ecstasy. Then he finds his voice to say simply and everlastingly, "my son."

978-0-595-37461-8
0-595-37461-1

Made in the USA
Monee, IL
13 November 2022

17682644R00111